Prisoners' Rights

POINT // COUNTERPOINT

Prisoners' Rights

David L. Hudson, Jr.

SERIES CONSULTING EDITOR
Alan Marzilli, M.A., J.D.

CHELSEA HOUSE
PUBLISHERS
An imprint of Infobase Publishing

Prisoners' Rights

Chelsea House
An imprint of Infobase Publishing
132 West 31st Street
New York, NY 10001

Library of Congress Cataloging-in-Publication Data

Hudson, David L., 1969–
  Prisoners' rights / David L. Hudson, Jr.
    p. cm. — (Point/counterpoint)
  Includes bibliographical references and index.
  ISBN-13: 978-0-7910-9277-4 (hardcover)
  ISBN-10: 0-7910-9277-1 (hardcover)
  1. Prisoners—Civil rights—United States. 2. Prisoners—Legal status, laws, etc.—United States. I. Title. II. Series.

  HV9471.H83 2007
  323.3'29270973—dc22   2007003603

Chelsea House books are available at special discounts when purchased in bulk quantities for businesses, associations, institutions, or sales promotions. Please call our Special Sales Department in New York at (212) 967-8800 or (800) 322-8755.

You can find Chelsea House on the World Wide Web at
http://www.chelseahouse.com

Series design by Keith Trego
Cover design by Ben Peterson

Printed in the United States of America

Bang Hermitage 10 9 8 7 6 5 4 3 2 1

This book is printed on acid-free paper.

All links and Web addresses were checked and verified to be correct at the time of publication. Because of the dynamic nature of the Web, some addresses and links may have changed since publication and may no longer be valid.

CONTENTS

Foreword
Alan Marzilli, M.A., J.D.
Washington, D.C.

The debates presented in POINT/COUNTERPOINT are among the most interesting and controversial in contemporary American society, but studying them is more than an academic activity. They affect every citizen; they are the issues that today's leaders debate and tomorrow's will decide. The reader may one day play a central role in resolving them.

Why study both sides of the debate? It's possible that the reader will not yet have formed any opinion at all on the subject of this volume—but this is unlikely. It is more likely that the reader will already hold an opinion, probably a strong one, and very probably one formed without full exposure to the arguments of the other side. It is rare to hear an argument presented in a balanced way, and it is easy to form an opinion on too little information; these books will help to fill in the informational gaps that can never be avoided. More important, though, is the practical function of the series: Skillful argumentation requires a thorough knowledge of *both* sides—though there are seldom only two, and only by knowing what an opponent is likely to assert can one form an articulate response.

Perhaps more important is that listening to the other side sometimes helps one to see an opponent's arguments in a more human way. For example, Sister Helen Prejean, one of the nation's most visible opponents of capital punishment, has been deeply affected by her interactions with the families of murder victims. Seeing the families' grief and pain, she understands much better why people support the death penalty, and she is able to carry out her advocacy with a greater sensitivity to the needs and beliefs of those who do not agree with her. Her relativism, in turn, lends credibility to her work. Dismissing the other side of the argument as totally without merit can be too easy—it is far more useful to understand the nature of the controversy and the reasons *why* the issue defies resolution.

The most controversial issues of all are often those that center on a constitutional right. The Bill of Rights—the first ten amendments to the U.S. Constitution—spells out some of the most fundamental rights that distinguish the governmental system of the United States from those that allow fewer (or other) freedoms. But the sparsely worded document is open to interpretation, and clauses of only a few words are often at the heart of national debates. The Bill of Rights was meant to protect individual liberties; but the needs of some individuals clash with those of society as a whole, and when this happens someone has to decide where to draw the line. Thus the Constitution becomes a battleground between the rights of individuals to do as they please and the responsibility of the government to protect its citizens. The First Amendment's guarantee of "freedom of speech," for example, leads to a number of difficult questions. Some forms of expression, such as burning an American flag, lead to public outrage—but nevertheless are said to be protected by the First Amendment. Other types of expression that most people find objectionable, such as sexually explicit material involving children, are not protected because they are considered harmful. The question is not only where to draw the line, but how to do this without infringing on the personal liberties on which the United States was built.

The Bill of Rights raises many other questions about individual rights and the societal "good." Is a prayer before a high school football game an "establishment of religion" prohibited by the First Amendment? Does the Second Amendment's promise of "the right to bear arms" include concealed handguns? Is stopping and frisking someone standing on a corner known to be frequented by drug dealers a form of "unreasonable search and seizure" in violation of the Fourth Amendment? Although the nine-member U.S. Supreme Court has the ultimate authority in interpreting the Constitution, its answers do not always satisfy the public. When a group of nine people—sometimes by a five-to-four vote—makes a decision that affects the lives of hundreds of millions, public outcry can be expected. And the composition of the Court does change over time, so even a landmark decision is not guaranteed to stand forever. The limits of constitutional protection are always in flux.

These issues make headlines, divide courts, and decide elections. They are the questions most worthy of national debate, and this series aims to cover them as thoroughly as possible. Each volume sets out some of the key arguments surrounding a particular issue, even some views that most people consider extreme or radical—but presents a balanced perspective on the issue. Excerpts from the relevant laws and judicial opinions and references to central concepts, source material, and advocacy groups help the reader to explore the issues even further and to read "the letter of the law" just as the legislatures and the courts have established it.

It may seem that some debates—such as those over capital punishment and abortion, debates with a strong moral component—will never be resolved. But American history offers numerous examples of controversies that once seemed insurmountable but now are effectively settled, even if only on the surface. Abolitionists met with widespread resistance to their efforts to end slavery, and the controversy over that issue threatened to cleave the nation in two; but today public debate over the merits of slavery would be unthinkable, though racial inequalities still plague the nation. Similarly unthinkable at one time was suffrage for women and minorities, but this is now a matter of course. Distributing information about contraception once was a crime. Societies change, and attitudes change, and new questions of social justice are raised constantly while the old ones fade into irrelevancy.

Whatever the root of the controversy, the books in POINT/ COUNTERPOINT seek to explain to the reader the origins of the debate, the current state of the law, and the arguments on both sides. The goal of the series is to inform the reader about the issues facing not only American politicians, but all of the nation's citizens, and to encourage the reader to become more actively involved in resolving these debates, as a voter, a concerned citizen, a journalist, an activist, or an elected official. Democracy is based on education, and every voice counts—so every opinion must be an informed one.

Do the people behind bars deserve better treatment? The Unites States incarcerates more of its citizens than any other industrialized nation. The federal government estimates that about one out of every 20 people will eventually serve time in prison. Many people think that rising prison populations have forced inmates to live in substandard conditions. On the other hand, many crime victims and law enforcement officials believe that prisoners have too many rights. Historically, prisoners have turned to the court system to challenge prison conditions, but the overwhelming number of prisoner lawsuits in the late twentieth century led Congress to pass a law limiting the ability of inmates to sue in federal court. This volume examines the impact that the law has had.

One area in which inmates have seen their rights increase is in the area of religious liberty. Some of the same conservative politicians who favored limiting lawsuits by inmates also supported a federal law protecting prisoners' rights to religious worship and otherwise observing their religion through diet, dress, etc. The impact of this latter law is also examined. Finally, all of society, including prison systems, is experiencing rising medical costs. Although more money is going into health care in prisons, many charge that prisons provide inadequate care. The examination of these issues and discussion of some emerging issues provide a solid introduction to the topic of prisoners' rights.

Prisoners' Rights

Nearly a century ago, Sir Winston Churchill uttered the following words in making the point that a "most unfailing test of the civilization of any country" was how it treated its convicted criminals—its prison inmates:

> The mood and temper of the public in regard to the treatment of crime and criminals is one of the most unfailing tests of the civilization of any country. A calm and dispassionate recognition of the rights of the accused against the state, and even of convicted criminals against the state, a constant heart-searching by all charged with the duty of punishment . . . and an unaltering faith that there is a treasure, if you can only find it, in the heart of every man—these are the symbols which in the treatment of crime and criminals mark and measure the stored-up strength of a nation, and are the sign and proof of the living virtue in it.[1]

Many people view the phrase *prisoner rights* with bewil-derment. They find it inherently contradictory to talk about inmate rights. Some people believe prisoners forfeit their rights when they commit crimes. But the law recognizes a prisoner as a person, as someone who retains a certain level of basic human dignity.

Dignity may seem strange to inmates who face constant confinement, their liberty taken from them because they com-mitted crimes—perhaps awful crimes. Prisoners sometimes are isolated from others in administrative segregation or placed in "the hole" (prison slang for solitary confinement), where they have no contact with other human beings for 23 hours a day. Prison officials generally place inmates in the hole as a form of punishment for violating prison rules. Many times prisons go into a "lockdown" mode, during which inmates' movements are restricted while prison officials make sweeps for drugs and other contraband.

However, prisoners are people and they still retain some measure of constitutional freedoms. In the words of former U.S. Supreme Court Justice Sandra Day O'Connor, "Prison walls do not form a barrier separating inmates from the protections of the Constitution."[2] Such was not always the case in this country. For many years, a prison inmate was considered nothing more than a "slave of the state."[3] Prison officials could do almost anything to an inmate, with impunity.

In the first part of the twentieth century, the term *slave* generally was dropped but the concept remained the same—inmates had few constitutional rights or none at all. This period was called the "hands-off" period, meaning that courts did not get involved in overseeing prison administrative matters at this time. The courts kept their hands off the administrative duties of the prisons. Courts played virtually no role in the lives of prisons and prison officials.[4] Legal scholar Hedieh Nasheri reflects, "Because of the hands-off doctrine, even gross abuses were rarely brought to court."[5]

Even during the expansive period of constitutional rights during the 1960s heyday of the Warren Court (the U.S. Supreme Court when it was led by Chief Justice Earl Warren), prisons were often the last public institutions affected. The Court finally ruled that prisons must be desegregated in 1968—years after the Court had desegregated other public institutions.[6] The Supreme Court recognized the reach of the hands-off doctrine in 1974 when it wrote: "Traditionally, federal courts have adopted a broad hands-off doctrine toward problems of prison administration."[7]

In the 1960s and 1970s, however, the U.S. Supreme Court recognized that inmates do retain some level of constitutional rights while in prison. In *Cooper v. Pate*, the court reinstated a religious freedom lawsuit by an Illinois inmate who claimed he was denied his religious liberty rights because he was a black Muslim.[8] In *Johnson v. Avery* (1969), the court struck down a Tennessee prison policy that banned so-called jailhouse lawyers—inmates who helped other inmates file legal claims.[9] In the early 1970s, the Court reinstated a civil-rights lawsuit by a Buddhist inmate who alleged he was the victim of religious

FROM THE BENCH

Ruffin v. Commonwealth

A convicted felon, whom the law in its humanity punishes by confinement in the penitentiary instead of with death, is subject while undergoing that punishment, to all the laws which the Legislature in its wisdom may enact for the government of that institution and the control of its inmates. For the time being, during his term of service in the penitentiary, he is in a state of penal servitude to the State. He has, as a consequence of his crime, not only forfeited his liberty, but all his personal rights except those which the law in its humanity accords to him. He is for the time being the slave of the State. He is civiliter mortuus; and his estate, if he has any, is administered like that of a dead man.

Source: *Ruffin v. Commonwealth*, 62 Va. 790, 796-797 (1871).

What started as a small prisoner protest against substandard conditions at Attica Correctional Facility in Attica, New York, became a large-scale riot in September 1971. Above right, activist attorney William Kunstler announces to inmates that he has agreed to represent them at negotiations with prison officials.

discrimination.[10] These decisions all recognized that inmates possessed some level of constitutional rights.

Another event during this period caused national focus to spotlight prison conditions: the infamous prison riot in September 1971 at Attica Correctional Facility, a maximum-security prison near Buffalo, New York. The inmates at Attica were upset about poor medical care, mail censorship, overcrowding, and other shabby conditions. The inmates rebelled, taking numerous prison guards hostage and presenting authorities with a list of more than 30 demands. The inmates controlled the prison for five days, until New York governor Nelson Rockefeller ordered state police and National Guard troops to take the prison. During the ensuing struggle, 43 people died—33 inmates and 10 hostages.[11]

The Attica prison riot raised awareness of the prisoners' rights movement and called attention to deplorable conditions in many prisons. It also led to trials and investigations of prison rioters and law enforcement officials alike. Prisoner lawsuits followed. In January 2000, a settlement was finally reached, in which the Attica prisoners and their family members received $8 million in compensation.[12] Legal commentator Jessica Feierman explained, "Litigation is one of the few means by which prisoners can bring public attention to serious health and safety risks, including inadequate health care, widespread violence, sexual assault and unsafe environmental conditions."[13]

Two other legal developments fueled the rise of prisoner constitutional rights. The first concerned a more expansive Supreme Court interpretation of the Eighth Amendment of the Constitution. The second legal development was a law—usually called "Section 1983"—that concerned a broader reading of a

Legal Language: 42 U.S.C. § 1983

Every person who, under color of any statute, ordinance, regulation, custom, or usage, of any State or Territory or the District of Columbia, subjects, or causes to be subjected, any citizen of the United States or other person within the jurisdiction thereof to the deprivation of any rights, privileges, or immunities secured by the Constitution and laws, shall be liable to the party injured in an action at law, suit in equity, or other proper proceeding for redress, except that in any action brought against a judicial officer for an act or omission taken in such officer's judicial capacity, injunctive relief shall not be granted unless a declaratory decree was violated or declaratory relief was unavailable. For the purposes of this section, any Act of Congress applicable exclusively to the District of Columbia shall be considered to be a statute of the District of Columbia.

Source: 42 U.S.C. § 1983.

federal civil rights law, originally passed in 1866 after the Civil War to protect recently freed slaves.

The Eighth Amendment and "Evolving Standards of Decency"

The Eighth Amendment provides for the treatment of prisoners: "Excessive bail shall not be required, nor excessive fines imposed, nor cruel and unusual punishments inflicted." Traditionally, the Eighth Amendment has been applied to the death penalty—considering whether imposing the death penalty in a certain way (electrocution or lethal injection) or on a certain class of offenders (e.g., juveniles or mentally retarded inmates) is constitutional. In 1958, however, the Warren Court expanded the amendment's reach when it wrote that it "must draw its meaning from the evolving standards of decency that mark the progress of a maturing society."[14] That term—*evolving standards of decency*—means that society changes with respect to what it views as proper punishment for inmates.

The second major legal development that advanced the cause of prisoners' rights was the recognition that individuals could seek redress of their constitutional rights in federal courts through the statute called Section 1983. If an inmate believes that a prison official violated his religious liberty rights under the First Amendment, or his right to be free from unreasonable searches and seizures under the Fourth Amendment, or his right to be free from cruel and unusual punishment under the Eighth Amendment, the legal vehicle to carry those claims to court is Section 1983. The U.S. Supreme Court gave a broad reading to this statute in its 1961 decision *Monroe v. Pape*.[15]

Using Section 1983, prisoners began filing lawsuits challenging various aspects of their conditions of confinement. Many of their lawsuits challenged these aspects based on the Eighth Amendment and the "evolving standards of decency" prescription from the Warren Court. In the 1960s, prisoners successfully challenged the use of corporal punishment on inmates as cruel and unusual. The 8th U.S. Circuit Court of Appeals ruled in *Jackson v. Bishop* that whipping inmates violated the Eighth Amendment.[16]

The Supreme Court later clarified that physical abuse of an inmate can also constitute an Eighth Amendment violation even if the inmate does not suffer serious injury. In *Hudson v. McMillan* (1992), the Court ruled that Louisiana inmate Keith Hudson had a viable Eighth Amendment claim when he charged that officers had shackled him and punched him repeatedly. Justice O'Connor explained for the Court: "In the excessive force context, society's expectations are different. When prison officials maliciously and sadistically use force to cause harm, contemporary standards of decency are always violated. This is true whether or not significant injury is evident."[17] This decision was emphasized in 2002 when the Court ruled that Alabama prison officials violated the Eighth Amendment when they chained inmate Larry Hope to a hitching post for seven hours.[18]

FROM THE BENCH

Jackson v. Bishop

We are not convinced that any rule or regulation as to the use of the strap, however seriously or sincerely conceived and drawn, will successfully prevent abuse . . . corporal punishment is easily subject to abuse in the hands of the sadistic and the unscrupulous. Where power to punish is granted to persons in lower levels of administrative authority, there is an inherent and natural difficulty in enforcing the limitations of that power. There can be no argument that excessive whipping or the use of studded or overlong straps all constitute cruel and unusual punishment. But if whipping were to be authorized, how does one, or any court, ascertain the point which would distinguish the permissible from that which is cruel and unusual? Corporal punishment generates hate toward the keepers who punish and toward the system which permits it. It frustrates correctional and rehabilitative goals.

Source: *Jackson v. Bishop*, 404 F.2d 571 (8th Cir. 1968).

Deference to the Prison Administrator and Backlash Against Prisoner Rights

The prisoner rights movement and favorable decisions of the Warren Court gave way to a more conservative U.S. Supreme Court in the 1980s and beyond. The 1980s witnessed a diminishment of prisoners' constitutional rights, as the Court showed great deference to prison administrators. One commentator refers to the period from the 1980s to the present day as "the Deference Period."[19] An example of a case following this line of reasoning was *Turner v. Safley*, in 1987. In that decision, the Court ruled that prison regulations that impinge on constitutional rights are constitutional so long as they are reasonably related to legitimate penological (prison management) goals, such as inmate safety or rehabilitation.[20]

The *Turner v. Safley* standard for what is reasonable has four factors: First, there must be a "valid, rational connection" between the prison regulation and the legitimate governmental interest put forward to justify it.[21] A second factor relevant in determining the reasonableness of a prison restriction, as the case of *Pell v. Procunier* shows, is whether there are available alternative means a prisoner can use to exercise a particular constitutional right.[22] A third consideration is the impact that accommodating the asserted constitutional right will have on guards and other inmates, and on the allocation of prison resources generally.[23] As Justice O'Conner wrote in the majority opinion for *Turner*, "Finally, the absence of ready alternatives is evidence of the reasonableness of a prison regulation. . . . The existence of obvious, easy alternatives may be evidence that the regulation is not reasonable, but is an 'exaggerated response' to prison concerns."[24]

The reasonableness standard has held fast through the current Supreme Court. In recent years, the Court rejected the claims of a Montana inmate disciplined for helping another inmate with his legal materials.[25] The Court has also upheld a very restrictive visitation policy of the Michigan Department of

Corrections[26] and upheld a prison regulation in Pennsylvania that imposed very harsh restrictions on reading materials in a unit for inmates with discipline problems.[27]

Congressional Concern over Inmate Lawsuits and Protecting Religious Liberty

The reasonableness standard developed at a time when the U.S. Congress also clamped down on prisoner rights. Congress became concerned over the sheer number of inmate suits that were flooding the federal courts. Inmates were filing Section 1983 claims left and right, challenging various aspects of the conditions of their confinement. Some of the claims had merit, but many were believed to be frivolous. As a result, President Bill Clinton signed the Prison Litigation Reform Act (PLRA), which places limits on prisoner lawsuits, in 1996.

The one possible exception to this pattern of lesser protection for inmates and greater deference to administrators occurred in the area of religious liberty. Congress did pass two laws—the 1993 Religious Freedom Restoration Act and the 2000 Religious Land Use and Institutionalized Persons Act—which

FROM THE BENCH

Turner v. Safley

Subjecting the day-to-day judgments of prison officials to an inflexible strict scrutiny analysis would seriously hamper their ability to anticipate security problems and to adopt innovative solutions to the intractable problems of prison administration. The rule would also distort the decision-making process, for every administrative judgment would be subject to the possibility that some court somewhere would conclude that it had a less restrictive way of solving the problem at hand. Courts inevitably would become the primary arbiters of what constitutes the best solution to every administrative problem, thereby "unnecessarily perpetuat[ing] the involvement of the federal courts in affairs of prison administration."

Source: *Turner v. Safley,* 482 U.S. 78, 89 (1987).

put a greater burden on prison officials who were curtailing inmates' religious freedoms.

———————•————————•————————•———————

Summary

This book examines several pressing issues in the area of prisoner rights and presents both sides of this divisive debate. In particular it examines the controversial Prisoner Litigation Reform Act, religious-liberty rights of inmates, and medical care for inmates. The first two chapters, on the PLRA, examine whether Congress was justified in imposing limits on when prisoners can access the courts or whether Congress went too far. Congress had legitimate concerns about frivolous lawsuits, but some critics contend that the resulting legislation also threatens many valid lawsuits.

The third and fourth chapters examine the issue of religious liberty in prisons. Congress and the U.S. Supreme Court have been sparring over this area since at least 1990. Essentially, Congress believed that the U.S. Supreme Court gave short shrift to the Free Exercise Clause of the First Amendment in one of its decisions. Congress responded by passing federal laws that gave more individual protection for religious liberty. Because inmates are subject to the greatest type of governmental control, Congress specifically included inmates within the purview of these laws. Some believe that inmates now use and abuse these religious liberty laws and hide behind religion to circumvent prison rules. Others contend that religious freedom should be protected for inmates because religion is key to rehabilitation.

The two chapters that follow the religious liberty debate tackle another controversial concept: health care in prisons and jails. The reality is that society is incarcerating inmates at a higher rate than ever before in the nation's history. This has placed intense burdens on already understaffed prison medical facilities.

The result has been catastrophic in some cases, with tragic and perhaps preventable inmate deaths. In order to manage increasing demands for medical care, many states have contracted with private health care companies. Critics allege that some of those private companies place profit far above prisoner health.

These are not the only controversies involving prisoner rights, but they are some of the more pressing issues. It is hoped that this book will open eyes and cause real debate and critical thinking regarding prisoner rights.

It Is Reasonable to Place Limits on Prisoner Lawsuits

A Texas inmate sued the state's department of criminal justice because they did not provide him with a ladder to access the top bunk bed in his prison cell.[28] A Pennsylvania inmate sued prison officials in federal court because the prison sold individual packs of hot cocoa for 30 cents instead of providing them for free.[29] An inmate in Michigan sued prison officials in federal court because the officials served him and other Muslim inmates peanut butter and jelly sandwiches at nighttime during the religious holiday of Ramadan.[30] Even though state or federal courts rejected all three of these claims as frivolous, they took up valuable time and resources on the part of prison officials, government attorneys, and the courts.

These three claims are not that unusual in the world of prisoner litigation. Inmates have sued for insufficient locker space, a bad haircut by a prison barber, the failure to be invited to a pizza party for a departing prison employee, and being served the wrong kind of peanut butter.[31] Still other claims have included a lack of shampoo, the refusal of permission to use a photocopying machine, a male inmate's right to wear a bra, and the denial of a second serving of ice cream.[32]

The sheer number of prisoner lawsuits caused a flood of litigation in the federal courts in the latter half of the twentieth century. Prisoner lawsuits rose in frequency in the 1960s and even more in the 1970s due to some favorable U.S. Supreme Court decisions. Then in the late 1980s and early 1990s—partly due to a sharp increase in the prison population—there were even more prisoner lawsuits. According to the Administrative Office of the U.S. Courts, there were more than 41,000 prisoner lawsuits filed in federal district courts in 1996.[33] This led to the passage of the Prison Litigation Reform Act. Some sources indicate that prisoner suits took up 15 percent of the federal court's docket.[34] Another source listed that fraction as 25 percent.[35] Whatever the exact number, the undeniable reality was that federal inmate suits were clogging the federal courts, taking up precious time that could have been afforded to claims with merit. This is not to suggest that there are no meritorious, or valid, prisoner lawsuits. Certainly, a few of them are valid. But, as legal commentator Eugene J. Kuzinski has written, "the problem is that meritorious claims are the exception, rather than the rule."[36]

The Prison Litigation Reform Act serves the valid purpose of reducing frivolous inmate suits.

For the aforementioned reasons and others, Congress passed the Prison Litigation Reform Act (PLRA) in 1996. President Bill Clinton signed the measure into law in April 1996. The PLRA seeks to reduce the number of frivolous inmate suits and to weed out many of these claims before the federal government expends resources to deal with them. Speaking in support of the legislation, Senator Bob Dole stated in Congress that, "prisons should be just that—prisons, not law firms."[37]

The PLRA provides that inmates must use up their administrative remedies in prison before they can file a lawsuit in federal court. This means that the inmate must first complain through the appropriate channels in the prison system. The PLRA provides: "No action shall be brought with respect to prison conditions under section 1983 of this title, or any other Federal law,

Senator Robert Dole on Inmate Litigation

Unfortunately, the litigation explosion now plaguing our country does not stop at the prison gate. According to Enterprise Institute scholar Walter Berns, the number of "due-process and cruel and unusual punishment" complaints filed by prisoners has grown astronomically—from 6,600 in 1975 to more than 39,000 in 1994. These suits can involve such grievances as insufficient locker space, a defective haircut by a prison barber, the failure of prison officials to invite a prisoner to a pizza party for a departing public employee, and yes, being served chunky peanut butter instead of the creamy variety. The list goes on and on.

These legal claims may sound far-fetched, almost funny, but unfortunately, prisoner litigation does not operate in a vacuum. Frivolous lawsuits filed by prisoners tie up the courts, waste valuable legal resources, and affect the quality of justice enjoyed by law-abiding citizens. The time and money spent defending these cases are clearly time and money better spent prosecuting violent criminals, fighting illegal drugs, or cracking down on consumer fraud.

The National Association of Attorneys General estimates that inmate civil rights litigation costs the States more than $81 million each year. Of course, most of these costs are incurred defending lawsuits that have no merit whatsoever.

Let me be more specific. According to the Arizona Attorney General Grant Woods, a staggering 45 percent of the civil cases filed in Arizona's federal courts last year were filed by state prisoners. That means that 20,000 prisoners in Arizona filed almost as many cases as Arizona's 3.5 million law-abiding citizens. And most of these prisoner lawsuits were filed free of charge. No courts costs. No filing fees. This is outrageous and it must stop.

Source: 141 Cong. Rec. S14413 (September 27, 2005), http://frwebgate.access.gpo.gov/cgi-bin/getpage.cgi?dbname=1995_record&position=all&page=S14413 (accessed January 5, 2007).

by a prisoner confined in any jail, prison, or other correctional facility until such administrative remedies as are available are exhausted."[38] This provision of the PLRA gives prison officials the time to address and perhaps correct problems before they ever reach the lawsuit stage. Senator Orrin Hatch (R.-Utah)

Senator Orrin Hatch

Our legislation also addresses the flood of frivolous lawsuits brought by inmates. In 1994, over 39,000 lawsuits were filed by inmates in Federal courts, a staggering 15 percent over the number filed the previous year. The vast majority of these suits are completely without merit. Indeed, roughly 94.7 percent are dismissed before the pretrial phase, and only a scant 3.1 percent have enough validity to even reach trial. In my own home State of Utah, 297 inmate suits were filed in Federal courts during 1994, which accounted for 22 percent of all Federal civil cases filed in Utah last year. I should emphasize that these numbers do not include habeas corpus petitions or other cases challenging the inmate's conviction or sentence. The crushing burden of these frivolous suits makes it difficult for the courts to consider meritorious claims.

Indeed, I do not want to prevent inmates from raising legitimate claims. This legislation will not prevent those claims from being raised. The legislation will, however, go far in preventing inmates from abusing the Federal judicial system. In one frivolous case in Utah, for example, an inmate sued demanding that he be issued Reebok or L.A. Gear brand shoes instead of the Converse brand being issued. In another case, an inmate deliberately flooded his cell and then sued the officers who cleaned up the mess because they got his pinochle cards wet. And in a third case, from Utah, a prisoner sued officers after a cell search, claiming that they failed to put his cell back in a fashionable condition, and mixed his clean and dirty clothes....

It is time to stop this ridiculous waste of taxpayers' money. The huge costs imposed on State governments to defend against these meritless suits is another kind of crime committed against law-abiding citizens.

Source: 141 Cong. Rec. 14626-14627 (September 29, 2005) http://frwebgate2.access.gpo.gov/cgi-bin/waisgate.cgi?WAISdocID=386857303917+0+0+0&WAISaction=retrieve (accessed January 5, 2007).

explained that the intent is not to thwart legitimate complaints from prisoners. He even stated on the Senate floor that he did not want to prevent such claims. His point was that the "crushing burden of these frivolous suits makes it difficult for the courts to consider meritorious claims."[39]

The PLRA has had a positive effect in reducing the number of inmate suits. The Bureau of Justice Statistics reported in a detailed study that the number of prisoner suits declined substantially after the passage of the PLRA. The report notes that inmates filed 41,679 petitions in 1995 (the year before the PLRA was passed) and only 25,504 during 2000.[40] Another report reaches similar findings: "The Prison Litigation Reform Act has produced a significant reduction in the number of prisoner lawsuits coming to the federal courts" and "clearly, the goal of reducing the share of federal judicial workload devoted to prisoner litigation has been achieved."[41]

The PLRA prevents courts from micromanaging prisons.

> The second major part of the Prison Litigation Reform Act establishes some tough new guidelines for Federal courts when evaluating legal challenges to prison conditions. These guidelines will work to restrain liberal Federal judges who see violations on constitutional rights in every prisoner complaint and who have used these complaints to micromanage state and local prison systems.[42]
>
> — Senator Robert Dole

A second major part of the PLRA imposes greater burdens on courts when they attempt to micromanage prisons. Legal scholar Eugene Kuzinski wrote, "From the perspective of state officials, and many in Congress, federal judges have in some instances literally seized control of entire state correctional systems."[43] Some federal judges imposed orders on state prison systems that gave the federal judges complete oversight of state prison policies. A federal judge in Philadelphia had control over pretrial bail policies at the prison for a decade, which led to the release of many criminals who went out and committed more crimes.[44]

The PLRA limits when courts can issue "prospective relief," or relief in the future. The law provides that a court "shall not grant or approve any prospective relief unless the court finds that such relief is narrowly drawn, extends no further than necessary to correct the violation of the Federal right, and is the least intrusive means necessary to correct the violation of the Federal right."[45] The law also contains a "termination of relief" provision. Under this provision, prison officials can petition to end court supervision unless the court supplies new, written

FROM THE BENCH

Justice Clarence Thomas

State prisons should be run by the state officials with the expertise and the primary authority for running such institutions. Absent the most extraordinary circumstances, federal courts should refrain from meddling in such affairs. Prison administrators have a difficult enough job without federal court intervention. An overly broad remedial decree can make an already daunting task virtually impossible.

I realize that judges, "no less than others in our society, have a natural tendency to believe that their individual solutions to often intractable problems are better and more workable than those of the persons who are actually charged with and trained in the running of the particular institution under examination." But, judges occupy a unique and limited role, one that does not allow them to substitute their views for those in the executive and legislative branches of the various States, who have the constitutional authority and institutional expertise to make these uniquely nonjudicial decisions and who are ultimately accountable for these decisions. Though the temptation may be great, we must not succumb. The Constitution is not a license for federal judges to further social policy goals that prison administrators, in their discretion, have declined to advance.

Source: *Lewis v. Casey,* 518, 387-388 U.S. 343 (1996) (J. Thomas, concurring).

In the photo above, inmates at California's Deuel Vocational Institute are housed in three-tier bunks in what was once a multipurpose recreational room. As in detention facilities throughout the country, overcrowding forced Deuel to construct temporary housing.

findings that clearly show the need for the oversight and relief to continue. One provision, called the "automatic stay" provision, provides that prospective relief will be stayed, or halted, pending the resolution of the legal challenge to end such relief. The proposal places a 90-day deadline on federal judges to consider whether to end court monitoring of prison conditions.

The U.S. Supreme Court upheld the constitutionality of this provision in *Miller v. French*.[46] Writing for the majority of the court, Justice O'Connor reasoned, "the stay merely reflects the changed legal circumstances—that prospective relief under the existing decree is no longer enforceable, and remains unenforceable unless and until the court makes the findings required by § 3626(b)(3) [another provision in the law]."[47] She concluded, "the PLRA does not deprive courts of their adjudicatory role, but merely provides a new legal standard for relief and encourages courts to apply that standard promptly."[48]

The PLRA reasonably restricts inmate suits in other ways.

The PLRA also imposes reasonable limits on inmates in terms of the costs of filing lawsuits. In the past, inmates could file suits and claim indigent status—that is, inability to pay legal costs due to lack of finances. Senator Dole spoke of this when introducing the PLRA in Congress, saying that most of these "outrageous" prisoner suits were filed free of cost. Under the PLRA, inmates must pay court costs in full. It provides that, if inmates cannot

THE LETTER OF THE LAW

Automatic Stay Provision in the PLRA

(e) Procedure for Motions Affecting Prospective Relief.—
(1) Generally.— The court shall promptly rule on any motion to modify or terminate prospective relief in a civil action with respect to prison conditions. Mandamus [an order from a superior court to a lower court or government official] shall lie to remedy any failure to issue a prompt ruling on such a motion.
(2) Automatic stay.— Any motion to modify or terminate prospective relief made under subsection (b) shall operate as a stay during the period—
(A)
(i) beginning on the 30th day after such motion is filed, in the case of a motion made under paragraph (1) or (2) of subsection (b); or
(ii) beginning on the 180th day after such motion is filed, in the case of a motion made under any other law; and
(B) ending on the date the court enters a final order ruling on the motion.
(3) Postponement of automatic stay.— The court may postpone the effective date of an automatic stay specified in subsection (e)(2)(A) for not more than 60 days for good cause. No postponement shall be permissible because of general congestion of the court's calendar.

Source: 18 U.S.C. § 3626(e)(1)-(3), http://www.law.cornell.edu/uscode/html/uscode18/usc_sec_18_00003626----000-.html (accessed January 5, 2007).

pay the court filing costs up front, the inmate can pay 20 percent of either "the average monthly deposits to the prisoner's account; or the average monthly balance in the prisoner's account for the 6-month period immediately preceding the filing of the complaint or notice of appeal."[49] The law does provide an exception for prisoners who truly are too poor to afford the costs: "In no event shall a prisoner be prohibited from bringing a civil action or appealing a civil or criminal judgment for the reason that the prisoner has no assets and no means by which to pay the initial partial filing fee."[50]

Another provision deals with those inmates who repeatedly file frivolous lawsuits. The law contains a three-strikes clause, preventing access to the courts by inmates who are serial filers, or those who have filed three frivolous or malicious claims in the past. Unfortunately, some inmates are "serial filers." In 2003, a federal district court in Georgia rejected the latest lawsuit by inmate Robert Heard because he had filed 17 lawsuits since 1990, most of which had been deemed frivolous.[51] One inmate named Clovis Carl Green Jr. filed nearly 500 lawsuits in state and federal courts in Missouri, Kansas, Minnesota, and Oklahoma.[52] A federal court in Missouri noted that "Inmate Green has not been content with the filing of hundreds of frivolous and malicious actions."[53] The PLRA was necessary to stop the abuses of serial filers such as Green.

Summary

Before the Prison Litigation Reform Act, inmates were besieging the courts with groundless claims. The federal courts should not be forced to contend with 20 to 25 percent of their claims coming from prisoners. These frivolous suits not only deplete resources, but also trivialize the valid claims that are filed by some prisoners. Something had to be done to rectify this situation.

In some locations, state prisons and local jails were additionally crippled by too much judicial oversight. Some federal judges had even established prison population caps, which meant the early release of dangerous criminals. Federal courts are important resources for the vindication of constitutional rights, but they should not be in the business of micromanaging prison systems.

Congress responded appropriately with the Prison Litigation Reform Act. It combats the problems caused by serial and frivolous filers and limits federal courts from micromanaging state prison systems.

The PLRA Deprives Inmates of Access to the Courts and Represents an Unconstitutional Power Grab by Congress

Ronald Nussle was an inmate serving time in a Connecticut prison. Nussle alleged that numerous prison officials subjected him to a prolonged period of harassment and abuse because he was perceived to be an ally of the state's governor, who had been feuding with correctional officers over labor issues. He alleged that several officers had come to his cell one day and beaten him severely. The officers warned him that if he reported the incident, they would take revenge with even further abuse.[54]

Nussle declined to file a grievance with the prison system for fear that the officers would retaliate. Instead, he sought refuge in the one place where inmates sometimes receive a fair shake—the federal courts. Unfortunately for Nussle, the courts rejected his claims because the Prison Litigation Reform Act (PLRA) required him to exhaust his administrative remedies first.[55] The U.S. Supreme Court determined in *Porter v. Nussle* that the "PLRA's exhaustion requirement applies to all inmate suits about prison life, whether they involve general circumstances or particular episodes, and whether they allege excessive force or some other wrong."[56]

The net effect of this U.S. Supreme Court ruling is that many valid inmate suits are prevented from ever being heard by an impartial federal judge. Inmates like Nussle face an impossible catch-22: report your grievance to prison officials and suffer physical harm in retaliation, or forever lose your right to sue. This is perhaps the greatest problem with the PLRA: It denies access to the courts for those whose basic human dignity has been beaten out of them.

Many inmate suits are meritorious, rather than frivolous.

When introducing the Prison Litigation Reform Act, several members of Congress recited a laundry list of prisoner lawsuits that they characterized as frivolous. These included cases in which inmates sued for the delivery of the wrong pair of tennis shoes, the wrong type of peanut butter, and similar, seemingly trivial matters. This does not paint an accurate picture of prisoner litigation. Many inmates' suits are legitimate, meritorious complaints designed to address the deprivation of fundamental constitutional rights. Inmates have sued over brutal rapes by prison guards, vicious physical assaults, rat infestations, and prison cells soaked by overflowing toilets.[57] A female inmate sued after giving birth on the floor of her cell following three hours of labor with no medical attention. These suits were legitimate complaints.

One often-cited example of what is considered a frivolous inmate suit concerned a case brought by a prisoner over receiving the wrong kind of peanut butter. Unfortunately, the case was wrongly reported in the media and led to widespread public misperceptions. The case was not about the wrong type of peanut butter; instead, it was about the prison's failure to return $2.50 to the inmate's account. Federal appeals court Judge Jon

O. Newman wrote in *Newsweek*: "the unfair loss of $2.50 might not seem like much, but it is not trivial to a prisoner with limited funds. Though some prisoner—and nonprisoner—suits are frivolous, we ought not to ridicule them all by perpetuating myths."[58] Legal commentator Jennifer Winslow agreed in a 2002 *UCLA Law Review* article: "While senators listed multitudinous examples of so-called frivolous and meritless prisoner lawsuits, little mention was made of meritorious suits, thus leaving the unknowing observer with the one-sided impression that all prisoner lawsuits must be merely 'recreational activity' for bored inmates."[59]

Unfortunately, that is what many supporters of the PLRA have done and continue to do—mischaracterize inmate suits as frivolous and try to lump all inmate suits together. Of course, there are some suits by inmates—and noninmates—that are frivolous. That does not mean that all inmate suits are frivolous. Many are meritorious and open the public's eyes to state

Legal Commentator Jennifer Winslow

Examination of the scope of the PLRA's provisions clearly reveals that the legislation was intended to be sweeping in its effect. Yet, Congress spent a remarkably short period of time debating the PLRA, and what little debate did occur was predominately one-sided. What emerged from the rhetoric was a sentiment that all inmate lawsuits are inherently frivolous and meritless. . . . PLRA proponents declared their intention to curtail the number of frivolous and meritless inmate suits clogging the federal judiciary. They then used exaggerated examples of inmate complaints to suggest subtly that all inmate suits are frivolous and meritless. While proponents provided assurances that meritorious inmate suits would not be affected by the PLRA, they made little effort to acknowledge that meritorious inmate suits do exist.

Source: Jennifer Winslow, "The Prison Litigation Reform Act's Physical Injury Requirement Bars Meritorious Lawsuits: Was It Meant To?" *UCLA Law Review* 49 (2002): 1655, 1658.

institutions—prisons, in this case—that are too often shrouded in secrecy.

Numerous provisions of the PLRA restrict inmates' fundamental right of access to the courts.

The undeniable purpose of the PLRA was to impose hurdles on inmates seeking to gain access to the federal courts for the vindication of their constitutional claims. The PLRA requires inmates to exhaust administrative remedies before filing suit in court. The law provides: "No action shall be brought with respect to prison conditions under section 1983 of this title, or any other Federal law, by a prisoner confined in any jail, prison, or other correctional facility until such administrative remedies as are available are exhausted."[60] As discussed with *Porter v. Nussle,* this provision does not provide adequate protection for those inmates who fear retaliation by prison officials if they blow the whistle on wrongdoing in the institution.

The PLRA also gives greater authority to judges to dismiss lawsuits that they deem frivolous or malicious, or that fail to state a legal claim.[61] This provision sounds reasonable, but what may be frivolous to a federal judge may not be frivolous to an inmate whose freedom is curtailed 24 hours a day. A judge may believe that a suit over the failure to credit $2.50 to an inmate's account is frivolous, but that may constitute a significant portion of an impoverished inmate's account. The meaning of *frivolous* is different for a free citizen than it is for an inmate.

Another provision of the PLRA states that inmates cannot recover monetary damages for suits unless they can show that they suffered some type of physical injury. This clause provides: "No Federal civil action may be brought by a prisoner confined in a jail, prison, or other correctional facility, for mental or emotional injury suffered while in custody without a prior showing of physical injury."[62] Commentator Deborah M. Golden warned that this provision "may prevent rape victims from bringing lawsuits against their attackers."[63] She wrote:

courts have dismissed cases involving inmates' nausea and vomiting, general bruising, bruised ribs, minor swelling, minor bleeding, abrasions and lacerations, skin fungus, dehydration, migraine headaches, increased blood pressure, aggravated hypertension, dizziness, insomnia, loss of appetite, burning eyes, shortness of breath, chest pain, mosquito bites resulting in fever, and the smell of cells smeared with feces rendering sleep impossible.[64]

Another legal commentator suggested that this provision "could bar inmates from recovering monetary damages for such violations as the denial of mental health care, racial discrimination, denial of religious freedoms, psychological torture, and retaliation for filing grievances."[65]

Yet another part of the PLRA imposes burdens upon prisoners who do not have the resources for legal fees. The law requires most inmates to pay court-filing fees in full. If an inmate does not have the money up front, the law allows the inmate to pay monthly installments through his or her commissary account.[66] A related provision prohibits an inmate who is classified as a "serial filer" from filing a claim in court. Such an inmate is one who previously has filed at least three suits that have been

Legal Language: The PLRA's Three-strikes Provision

In no event shall a prisoner bring a civil action or appeal a judgment in a civil action or proceeding under this section if the prisoner has, on 3 or more prior occasions, while incarcerated or detained in any facility, brought an action or appeal in a court of the United States that was dismissed on the grounds that it is frivolous, malicious, or fails to state a claim upon which relief may be granted, unless the prisoner is under imminent danger of serious physical injury.

Source: 28 U.S.C. § 1915g.

deemed frivolous or malicious. This is known as the three-strikes provision.[67]

The PLRA also severely limits the ability of courts to manage prison systems that may run rampant with abuse. Many times in the past, courts have had to take control and oversight over prisons to ensure that inmates were not subject to inhumane conditions. Sometimes the courts would obtain control following an agreement between prison officials and the plaintiffs in order to settle lawsuits. An agreement sometimes allowed long-term monitoring by the courts. The PLRA changes that, however, because Congress felt that some judges were micromanaging prisons. The net result is that inmates lose the best protection they could have had.

Traditionally, the federal judge has been the last line of defense for inmates. As former U.S. Supreme Court Justice William Brennan wrote 25 years ago: "Judicial intervention is indispensable if constitutional dictates—not to mention considerations of basic humanity—are to be observed in the prisons."[68] The PLRA takes control away from the judiciary by imposing new requirements on judges who seek to impose prospective relief, or relief extending into the future. For example, the law provides:

> Prospective relief in any civil action with respect to prison conditions shall extend no further than necessary to correct the violation of the Federal right of a particular plaintiff or plaintiffs. The court shall not grant or approve any prospective relief unless the court finds that such relief is narrowly drawn, extends no further than necessary to correct the violation of the Federal right, and is the least intrusive means necessary to correct the violation of the Federal right. The court shall give substantial weight to any adverse impact on public safety or the operation of a criminal justice system caused by the relief.[69]

Another provision prevents a court from entering prospective injunctive relief—for instance, an order preventing officials from engaging in certain practices pending the resolution of a lawsuit—unless the court makes detailed factual findings. The law provides that such relief will expire 90 days after its original entry.[70]

Another controversial part of the PLRA imposes an automatic stay, or halt—a 90-day deadline for federal judges to consider state officials' requests to end court monitoring and supervision of prison conditions. If the judge does not respond within the time period, then the state officials are freed from obligations.[71] The American Civil Liberties Union (ACLU) believes "this provision to be a blatant violation of the Constitution's separation of powers with respect to the legislative and judicial branches" because it "allows Congress to force federal judges to act within a time period mandated by Congress; and to take away judges' authority reversing their prior orders, if they fail to capitulate."[72] Donna Lennon of the ACLU wrote, "Congress is using the PLRA to dismantle court orders that remedy unconstitutional conditions."[73]

The PLRA ignores the fact that prison lawsuits help shed light on unconstitutional conditions in prisons.

The PLRA was enacted to reduce prisoner lawsuits while ignoring the fact that prisoner lawsuits often expose flagrant wrongdoings and harms in U.S. society. Prisons are the black holes of the government. The public often does not know what happens in these institutions. Consider the case of Alabama inmate Larry Hope, who was chained to a hitching post for at least seven hours with no bathroom breaks. The U.S. Supreme Court ruled in *Hope v. Pelzer* (2002) that this "obvious cruelty" violated the Eighth Amendment's prohibition against cruel and unusual punishment.[74]

Other inmate suits have shown that some correctional guards engage in sexual assaults on inmates, a practice that society should rightly condemn.[75] A federal court in New York ruled that state laws prohibiting sexual assaults by guards against inmates "demonstrate a national consensus that any sexual assault of a prisoner by a prison employee constitutes cruel and unusual punishment."[76] The inmate had a meritorious lawsuit that exposed a serious problem in the prison—sexual assaults by guards. Not all prisoner lawsuits are frivolous; many such lawsuits serve to highlight serious problems in society.

———————————•————————•————————•———————————

Summary

Many prisoner lawsuits have exposed inmate-on-inmate violence, guards' sexual rapes and assaults on inmates, other physical abuse of inmates, and terrible medical care in prisons. The PLRA treats prisoner claims with a very doubtful eye, imposing numerous procedural hurdles on the filing process. The law requires administrative grievances before prisoners can sue in court but ignores the reality that many prisoners fail to file such grievances because they fear harsh retaliation from prison officials and guards. In short, the PLRA restricts the fundamental right of inmates to access the courts.

William C. Collins

Some will argue that these events simply restore a more appropriate balance. After all, there are still constitutional protections for inmates that did not used to exist. Courts still find constitutional violations and order relief. But it certainly appears that the federal lawsuit as a vehicle for major prison reform is something whose heyday has passed. Is what remains enough to hold correctional institutions and agencies accountable for the care and treatment they provide inmates?

Source: William C. Collins, "Anatomy of the Modern Prisoners' Rights Suit: Bumps in the Road to the Courthouse: The Supreme Court and the Prison Litigation Reform Act," *Pace L. Rev.* 24 (2004): 651, 674.

Unfortunately, the law also severely limits the ability of the judicial system to address and correct violations of inmates' constitutional rights. Other parts of the PLRA represent a power grab by Congress to take control away from the federal judiciary. It has been the federal judiciary that has stopped many abuses in prisons, because federal judges are appointed to their positions for life and are therefore not subject to state and local pressures to rule a certain way. One commentator stresses that "injustices inflicted by government on the most despised persons especially call for an effective remedy."[77] The federal judiciary is often the last line of defense for those most in need of protection. Unfortunately, Congress turned a blind eye to this when it passed the PLRA. Many inmates are not protected from abuses because of this law.

Inmates Have Adequate Constitutional Protection for Religious Liberty

Inmate Harry Theriault, who had previously escaped from prisons on more than one occasion, founded a religion in the 1970s known as the Church of the New Song at a federal penitentiary in Atlanta, Georgia. Theriault obtained a doctorate in divinity from a mail order application and then declared himself to be the "Bishop of Tellus," ordained as a high minister. The church, headed by Theriault, served the needs of inmates in several prisons. Prison officials alleged that during so-called religious sessions, inmates used drugs and engaged in sexual acts. Prison officials alleged that the religion was a sham used by certain inmates to engage in other proscribable conduct. Theriault claimed that prison officials violated his rights of religious liberty when they restricted his activities.

A federal district court in Texas agreed with the rationale of the prison officials and rejected Theriault's claims, concluding:

The Church of the New Song appears not to be a religion, but rather as a masquerade designed to obtain First Amendment protection for acts which otherwise would be unlawful and/ or reasonably disallowed by the various prison authorities but for the attempts which have been and are being made to classify them as 'religious' and, therefore, presumably protected by the First Amendment.[78]

The court continued,

Rather than urging upon its followers any particular theology or philosophy of life, the Church of the New Song appears to encourage a relatively non-structured and free-form, do-as-you-please philosophy, the sole purpose of which is to cause or encourage disruption of established prison discipline for the sake of disruption.[79]

Many inmates use and abuse religion and the First Amendment in order to manipulate prison officials.

Theriault's case is not that unusual in the prison world. Numerous inmates claim religious exemptions from a vast assortment of prison tasks. Prisons must respect inmates' right to freely exercise some aspects of their religious faith, but there must be limits. For example, a white supremacist inmate in Iowa claimed he had a right to be housed with only white inmates. The inmate, who called himself a neo-Nazi skinhead, believed that his religious faith instructed him to live only with members of his own race. He sued prison officials after they housed him with an African-American inmate. A federal appeals court noted that it was doubtful that the inmate's "request to be racially segregated, first made in the midst of prison racial disturbances, reflected a sincerely held religious belief."[80] The inmate failed to explain "why this religion suddenly mandated that he no longer share his cell with an African-American."[81]

The federal appeals court concluded that the inmate's racist requests, disguised under the name of religion, must take a backseat to the prison officials' interests in institutional security. Prison officials must have broad leeway to determine how they want to lessen racial tensions without engaging in racial segregation. The court also pointed out that the prison could face a lawsuit if it segregated inmates based on race, because courts had previously ruled that prisons cannot be segregated.

Other inmates have alleged that their religious beliefs require them to have many conjugal visits—visits with their wives or girlfriends for purposes of sexual intercourse. For example, a federal prisoner in Illinois claimed that officials' denial of conjugal visits violated his rights to religious freedom. He further argued that because the nationwide prison population is disproportionately African American, the denial of conjugal visits to him as a black man constituted genocide. A federal appeals court rejected his claim.[82]

Inmates have even claimed that they have a First Amendment right to engage in drug use. For example, some inmates have contended that they have a religious liberty interest in smoking marijuana.

The U.S. Supreme Court has established a fair standard for evaluating free exercise of religion claims.

Inmates do not lose all of their constitutional rights in prison. They do retain a measure of their First Amendment rights to freely exercise their religious faith. For example, inmates may keep a copy of their religious text, such as the Bible or the Koran, in their cells. However, prison officials have broad leeway in policies designed to further legitimate safety concerns. In *O'Lone v. Estate of Shabazz* (1987), the U.S. Supreme Court established that prison regulations do not violate inmates' free exercise of religion rights under the First Amendment if the regulations are reasonably related to legitimate penological goals, such as safety or rehabilitation.[83]

O'Lone v. Estate of Shabazz involved policies enacted at Bayside State Prison in Leesburg, New Jersey, which required inmates to work outside for much of the day in groups. So-called gang minimum inmates had to work outside the main prison building. Because of the prison work detail schedules, many Muslim inmates could not attend Jumu'ah, an Islamic religious ceremony required to be held every Friday during daytime hours. Some Muslim inmates contended that these policies infringed upon their rights to free exercise of religion. The U.S. Supreme Court noted that "the very stringent requirements as to the time at which Juma'ah may be held make it extraordinarily

FROM THE BENCH

Chief Justice William Rehnquist

While we in no way minimize the central importance of Jumu'ah to respondents, we are unwilling to hold that prison officials are required by the Constitution to sacrifice legitimate penological objectives to that end. . . . Here, similarly, we think it appropriate to see whether under these regulations respondents retain the ability to participate in other Muslim religious ceremonies. The record establishes that respondents are not deprived of all forms of religious exercise, but instead freely observe a number of their religious obligations. The right to congregate for prayer or discussion is virtually unlimited except during working hours, and the state-provided imam has free access to the prison. Muslim prisoners are given different meals whenever pork is served in the prison cafeteria. Special arrangements are also made during the month-long observance of Ramadan, a period of fasting and prayer. During Ramadan, Muslim prisoners are awakened at 4:00 A.M. for an early breakfast, and receive dinner at 8:30 each evening. We think this ability on the part of respondents to participate in other religious observances of their faith supports the conclusion that the restrictions at issue here were reasonable. . . .

We take this opportunity to reaffirm our refusal, even where claims are made under the First Amendment to substitute our judgment on . . . difficult and sensitive matters of institutional administration.

Source: *O'Lone v. Estate of Shabazz*, 482 U.S. 342, 352-353 (1987).

difficult for prison officials to assure that every Muslim prisoner is able to attend that service."[84] The Court noted that accommodating the Muslim inmates would have placed a severe strain on prison officials and other inmates, and on prison resources generally.[85]

Federal laws provide too much protection to prisoner religious-liberty claims.

The *O'Lone* reasonableness standard works well in the prison setting. It gives prison officials a good deal of respect by considering their legitimate interests in safety and rehabilitation. It considers whether accommodating an inmate's religious request will impose hardships on prison resources or create a dangerous situation in which certain inmates are deemed to be the favorites of the guards, creating resentment among other inmates.

Congress stepped in and passed two laws that provide even more protection for inmates' religious liberty, however. The U.S. Supreme Court had a workable, rational, and basic reasonableness standard in place. Unfortunately, Congress passed two laws that increased the standard. These are the Religious Freedom Restoration Act of 1993 (RFRA)[86] and the Religious Land Use and Institutionalized Persons Act of 2000 (RLU-IPA).[87] Both laws impose a higher standard on federal, state, and local prison officials when they impinge upon an inmate's religious liberty rights. The laws provide that, if a prison regulation imposes a substantial burden on an inmate's religion, the law must further a strong governmental interest in the least restrictive way. This is the judicial standard known as strict scrutiny. It is a much higher standard than the reasonableness standard established by the U.S. Supreme Court in the *O'Lone* decision.

In 1997, the U.S. Supreme Court struck down the RFRA as it applied to state and local governments. The Court determined that the RFRA exceeded Congress's remedial powers under the

Fourteenth Amendment of the Constitution.[88] According to the Court, Congress overstepped its authority in imposing such a law upon the states. For this reason, Congress responded with the RLUIPA. Congress justified the RLUIPA under its spending and commerce clause powers, a protection it had failed to provide for the RFRA.

The net effect is that Congress has stepped in and passed laws that impose more burdens on prison officials with respect to inmates' religious-liberty claims. Law professor Marci Hamilton wrote that "it was unwise for Congress, with the RLUIPA, to increase the standard to 'strict scrutiny' review after the Court had wisely decided lower standards were proper."[89]

Another problem with the RLUIPA was that it created a very loose definition of religion. Legal commentator Morgan Johnson identified the RLUIPA's broad definition of "religious exercise" as "any exercise of religion, whether or not compelled by or central to a system of religious belief." Johnson wrote that this broad definition means that "any spiritual act is eligible for

Legal Commentator Morgan F. Johnson

There is no limit to the type or number of religious beliefs that prisoners can claim under RLUIPA; thus, there are few limits to the number of cases prisoners may bring under the statute. When prisoners realize that they may claim to be followers of any religion, regardless of its practices or creeds, and that they can demand special rights under RLUIPA, contrived religions may become commonplace in prisons because of the benefits religious prisoners receive. Consequently, by upholding RLUIPA's constitutionality, the Court has created a powerful weapon for religious groups.

Source: Morgan F. Johnson, "Heaven Help Us: The Religious Land Use and Institutionalized Persons Act's Prisoners Provisions in the Aftermath of the Supreme Court's Decision in Cutter v. Wilkinson," *American University Journal of Gender, Social Policy & the Law* 14 (2006): 585, 602.

protection."[90] She warned that this could create a floodgate of spurious religious-liberty claims by inmates.

One constitutional challenge filed against the RLUIPA was that it violated the Establishment Clause of the First Amendment, which is designed to ensure the separation of church and state. The argument made by Ohio prison officials was that the RLUIPA violated the Establishment Clause because it made prison officials favor religion in prison. For example, a lower federal court used the hypothetical example of two white supremacist inmates who both file a request for inflammatory, racist texts. One inmate says the material is necessary to practice his religion, while the other inmate just says that he is a skinhead and wants the material. Prison officials may have to give the material to the white supremacist inmate who made a religious request but not to the other inmate. The lower court noted that "the religious white supremacist now has a much better chance of success than the non-religious white supremacist, as prison officials bear the burden of proving that the prison policy satisfies a compelling interest and is the least restrictive means of satisfying the interest."[91]

Later, however, the U.S. Supreme Court rejected the Establishment Clause challenge to the RLUIPA in *Cutter v. Wilkinson* (2005).[92] The Court determined that the RLUIPA was a "permissible legislative accommodation of religion."[93]

The U.S. Supreme Court recognized that the RLUIPA must be interpreted in a way that accords respect to prison officials.

Even though the Court upheld the RLUIPA in the prison setting, it repeatedly recognized that the act should not be interpreted in a way that threatens prison security. "We do not read RLUIPA to elevate accommodation of religious observances over an institution's need to maintain order and safety," Justice Ruth Bader Ginsburg wrote for the majority. "Our decisions indicate that an accommodation must be measured so that it does not override other significant interests."[94] Justice Ginsburg also made the following statements in her decision:

(1) We have no cause to believe that RLUIPA would not be applied in an appropriately balanced way, with particular sensitivity to security concerns.[95]

(2) Lawmakers supporting RLUIPA were mindful of the urgency of discipline, order, safety, and security in penal institutions.[96]

Some people are concerned that the Court's decision upholding RLUIPA will lead to many more lawsuits by prisoners. Commentator Morgan Johnson wrote that the Court's decision in *Cutter* "will most likely result in an increase in litigation and thereby burden penological interests."[97]

Justice Ginsburg attempted to respond to such concerns in her opinion when she wrote: "We see no reason to anticipate that abusive prisoner litigation will overburden the operations of state and local institutions." She further noted that if "inmate requests for religious accommodations become excessive, impose unjustified burdens on other institutionalized persons, or jeopardize the effective functioning of an institution, the facility would be free to resist the imposition."[98]

Prison officials must be given broad leeway, particularly given the threat of radical Islam.

The terrorist strikes of September 11, 2001, seared the collective consciousness of Americans and many others worldwide. The terror attacks showed the dangers of radical Islamic terrorists who preach death to Israel and the United States. Unfortunately, radical Islam is a phenomenon that is alive and well in U.S. prisons. There is evidence that Richard Reid, the attempted "shoebomber," and Jose Padilla, the "dirty bomber," both arrested for attempted detonation of bombs, were influenced by radical Islam when they were in prison.[99] This presents a problem when there are more than 150,000 Muslim inmates in federal prisons nationwide. Charles Colson, a former Nixon aide who turned his life around through Christianity after his prison term, wrote: "I don't usually make predictions, but here's one I'll venture: If, God forbid, an attack by home-grown Islamist radicals occurs on American soil, many, if not most, of the perpetrators will have converted to Islam while in prison."[100]

This danger means that courts should give even more deference to prison administrators. The problem, however, is that if prison officials single out a group of radical Muslims, a reviewing court might view that as a violation of religious liberty. Legal commentator John Popeo recommended:

> Prisons need to implement regulatory measures which counteract the proliferation of radical Islam. However, there might be more efficient means to counteract the spread of terrorism within prisons. An option the BOP might consider is the employment of religious chaplains from as many sects as is feasible, and this might be accompanied with the careful monitoring and continuous physical observation of all chaplains throughout the provision of religious services.[101]

He also recommended that prison administrators seek out moderate Muslims "to assist them in their struggle to deter radical Islam" which he said "is imperative for both tactical public relation and policy reasons."[102]

Prisons should immediately identify imams or other religious leaders who preach outright terrorism and hatred for the United States. Prison should be a time for rehabilitation and religious liberty, not a breeding ground for terrorists. Prison administrators should be given leeway in determining the difference between religious exercise and outright subversion. Religious liberty is a vitally important constitutional right, but nothing is more important than national security.

Summary

Religious liberty is important in the United States. It has turned around the lives of many inmates, including Malcolm X and Chuck Colson. Some inmates, however, use and abuse religion in the prison system. They use religion to seek exemptions from all sorts of general prison regulations. They abuse the legal system with frivolous lawsuits. Inmates do not have a religious right to conjugal visits, to use illegal drugs in prison, or to impose their racist beliefs on officers making cell assignments.

The U.S. Supreme Court has established a sound framework for evaluating inmate religious-liberty claims. This reasonableness standard takes into account how accommodating the inmate would impact other inmates and prison officials. It mandates looking for a less restrictive way of accommodating the inmate. Congress has stepped in and imposed greater burdens on prison officials with the Religious Land Use and Institutionalized Persons Act. Although the Supreme Court emphasized that the new law should not take away from the traditional deference owed to prison officials, only time will tell how the new law will affect prison officials and institutional security.

Inmates' Religious-liberty Rights Are Fundamental and Must Be Protected

Billy Soza Warsoldier, a Cahuilla Native American, served time in a minimum security prison in California. Warsoldier's religion required him to never cut his hair, which is believed to be a man's source of strength and wisdom. He also believed that cutting his hair would harm his chances of an afterlife. His religion's practices provided that one could not cut one's hair except when a family member died. Warsoldier adhered to this religious tenet, and had cut his hair only once since 1971—when his father died in 1980.[103]

The California Department of Corrections had a grooming policy that prohibited inmates from keeping their hair longer than three inches. Warsoldier refused to comply with this policy. Prison officials punished him for refusing to cut his hair. They took away his preferred job assignment, took away his phone privileges, expelled him from print shop and landscaping classes, removed him from the Executive Body for the Inmate Advisory Council and prohibited him from going to the main yard during recreation time.[104]

Warsoldier contended that prison officials violated his rights to religious liberty under the federal law put forth by the Religious Land Use and Institutionalized Persons Act. He contended that prison officials should have granted him a religious exemption from the grooming policy. Prison officials countered that they had several compelling interests in the policy. They said the policy allowed identification of prisoners, saying that a prisoner could escape and then alter his appearance by cutting his hair. They also told the court that inmates could hide contraband in long hair; that grooming policies reduce animosities by removing a method for inmates to convey gang affiliations; that short hair reduces injuries with the use of heavy machinery; and that short hair reduces the chances of lice.[105]

The 9th U.S. Circuit Court of Appeals ruled in favor of Warsoldier, finding that prison officials had failed to show that they had ever considered a less restrictive policy than their current one. The appeals court noted that one alternative "would be the creation of a religious exemption."[106] According to the court, other prison systems—including the federal system and the systems in Nevada, Colorado, and Utah—all granted religious exemptions from grooming policies and did not experience resulting problems. "Surely these other state and federal prison systems have the same compelling interests in maintaining prison security, ensuring public safety, and protecting inmate health as CDC [the California Department of Corrections]," the court wrote. "Nevertheless, CDC offers no explanation why these prison systems are able to meet their indistinguishable interests without infringing on their inmates' right to freely exercise their religious beliefs."[107]

The appeals court also pointed out that the CDC failed to impose a similar grooming policy on female inmates. "Concerns about inmate identification, lice infestation, and the ease with which an escaped inmate may alter his or her appearance are the same regardless of the sex of the offender," the court wrote.[108]

The court concluded that the CDC violated federal law by punishing Warsoldier for exercising his religious beliefs. The decision establishes that inmates do not lose all of their constitutional rights when they enter prison. They retain some level of constitutional rights and basic human dignity.

Religious freedom is a vitally important constitutional right for inmates.

Freedom of religion is vitally important for prisoners who are confined 24 hours a day, 365 days a year. One goal of prison is rehabilitation, and religion can be a key factor in becoming rehabilitated. Chuck Colson is living proof of the importance of religion to an inmate. Colson, a former aide to President Richard Nixon, pleaded guilty in 1974 to obstruction of justice and received a three-year sentence. Colson was a hatchet man who did much of Nixon's political dirty work. For his crime, he served seven months in an Alabama prison. The prison experience gave Colson time to reflect on his life and his ways. In prison, Colson converted to Christianity and changed his life and that of thousands of other inmates forever. In the words of one journalist, Colson went from "preying to praying."[109] He later founded a Christian-based organization known as Prison Fellowship Ministries, which, he said, "has become the world's largest outreach to prisoners, ex-prisoners, crime victims, and their families."[110]

Another example of the power of religion was a small-time criminal named Malcolm Little, who discovered the power of Islam in prison. When Little left prison, he left behind his old ways and changed his name to Malcolm X. He would go on to become an icon and worldwide religious leader, and would contribute greatly to the growth of the civil rights movement in the United States.[111]

Countless other inmates started a new path in life because of religion. Even for inmates serving a life sentence or sitting on

A Muslim inmate talks with a Muslim corrections officer after weekly worship at Rikers Island jail complex in New York. At Rikers, the room shown above is used as a mosque for Muslim worship. Most prisons attempt to make accommodations to enable inmates to exercise their religious liberties.

death row, religion can have a profound, positive influence on their lives. It can be essential to physical and mental survival. For this reason, the courts should take special care in protecting the religious-freedom rights of inmates.

The U.S. Supreme Court has established that inmates have religious-liberty rights.

The U.S. Supreme Court has recognized that inmates retain First Amendment rights to freely exercise their religious faith. In 1964, the court rejected the hands-off approach and determined that the First Amendment applies in prisons. In *Cooper v. Pate*, the Court addressed a case in which an Illinois inmate, Thomas

Cooper, alleged that he was denied permission to purchase religious publications of the Black Muslim movement. Cooper alleged that he was the victim of discrimination based on his religious beliefs because other inmates could obtain Christian Bibles while he was not able to obtain a copy of the Koran. Lower federal courts rejected Cooper's claims, saying that incarceration brings about the loss of many constitutional rights and privileges.[112] Cooper appealed to the U.S. Supreme Court, which reversed the lower court rulings and reinstated Cooper's lawsuit. "Taking as true the allegations of the complaint, as they must be on a motion to dismiss, the complaint stated a cause of action and it was error to dismiss it."[113]

The Supreme Court again protected inmate freedom of religion rights in *Cruz v. Beto*, which involved a Texas inmate named Fred Cruz who alleged that prison officials discriminated against Buddhism.[114] Cruz alleged that prison officials placed him in solitary confinement after he attempted to pass out Buddhist religious literature. He also alleged that prison officials prohib-

FROM THE BENCH

Cruz v. Beto

Federal courts sit not to supervise prisons but to enforce the constitutional rights of all persons, including prisoners. We are not unmindful that prison officials must be accorded latitude in the administration of prison affairs, and that prisoners necessarily are subject to appropriate rules and regulations. But persons in prison, like other individuals, have the right to petition the Government for redress of grievances which, of course, includes access of prisoners to the courts for the purpose of presenting their complaints. . . . If Cruz was a Buddhist and if he was denied a reasonable opportunity of pursuing his faith comparable to the opportunity afforded fellow prisoners who adhere to conventional religious precepts, then there was palpable discrimination by the State against the Buddhist religion, established in 600 B.C., long before the Christian era.

Source: *Cruz v. Beto*, 405 U.S. 319, 321-322 (1972).

ited him from communicating with his religious adviser of the Buddhist faith. Lower courts had rejected Cruz's claims based on the traditional rationale that courts should defer to the reasonable judgment of prison administrators. The U.S. Supreme Court reinstated Cruz's claims, finding that his allegations, if true, violated the First Amendment.

Congress has provided much-needed protection to prisoners by passing the RLUIPA.

When the Supreme Court recognized that inmates do not lose all of their First Amendment rights in prison, the Court also established a very low standard for prison officials to meet in its 1987 decisions *Turner v. Safley*[115] and *O'Lone v. Estate of Shabazz*.[116] In these decisions, the Court determined that prison regulations that affect inmates' constitutional rights are constitutional if they are reasonably related to legitimate penological concerns, such as safety or rehabilitation.[117] This standard generally led lower courts to reject inmates' First Amendment claims. Then, in 1990, the U.S. Supreme Court lowered the level of protection for free exercise of religion claims in general in *Employment Division v. Smith*.[118] Although the case did not involve inmates, it established that the Free Exercise Clause is not violated as long as a law generally applies across the board and does not target a specific religious faith. This meant that all people, including prisoners, had very little protection to freely exercise their religious faith.

Congress responded to this decision with the Religious Freedom Restoration Act in 1993 and the Religious Land Use and Institutionalized Persons Act in 2000. The RLUIPA provides a great deal of religious-liberty protection to inmates. The act expands inmates' religious-freedom rights because it imposes a higher standard on prison officials. Under the RLUIPA, prison officials cannot "impose a substantial burden" on an inmate's religious practices unless the government can show that its regulation advances a compelling government interest in the least restrictive way. This is the standard known in legal circles as "strict scrutiny."

Many members of Congress supported the RLUIPA because they recognized that inmates need religious freedom protection. Senator Orrin Hatch, a conservative Republican from Utah, and Senator Edward Kennedy, a liberal Democrat from Massachusetts, joined forces on this issue to ensure that the RLUIPA passed through Congress. In a joint statement in Congress, Hatch and Kennedy stated:

> Congress has long acted to protect the civil rights of institutionalized persons. Far more than any other Americans, persons residing in institutions are subject to the authority of one or a few local officials. Institutional residents' right to practice their faith is at the mercy of those running the insti-

Legal Language: RLUIPA

(a) General rule
No government shall impose a substantial burden on the religious exercise of a person residing in or confined to an institution, as defined in section 1997 of this title, even if the burden results from a rule of general applicability, unless the government demonstrates that imposition of the burden on that person—
   (1) is in furtherance of a compelling governmental interest; and
   (2) is the least restrictive means of furthering that compelling governmental interest.

(b) Scope of application
This section applies in any case in which—
   (1) the substantial burden is imposed in a program or activity that receives Federal financial assistance; or
   (2) the substantial burden affects, or removal of that substantial burden would affect, commerce with foreign nations, among the several States, or with Indian tribes.

Source: 42 U.S.C. § 2000cc-1.

tution, and their experience is very mixed. It is well known that prisoners often file frivolous claims; it is less well known that prison officials sometimes impose frivolous or arbitrary rules. Whether from indifference, ignorance, bigotry, or lack of resources, some institutions restrict religious liberty in egregious and unnecessary ways.[119]

Senators Hatch and Kennedy recognized that prisoners needed special protection because their lives are controlled by government officials more than any others. Many critics focus on a few strange lawsuits filed by prisoners, but—as the senators said—few focus on the frivolous or arbitrary rules sometimes imposed on prisoners by prison officials. The RLUIPA changed that equation.

The U.S. Supreme Court upheld the RLUIPA in its 2005 decision *Cutter v. Wilkinson.*[120] The case involved the claims of several inmates from nonmainstream religions, such as Wicca, Satanism, Asatru, and the Church of Jesus Christ Christian (a white supremacist group). The inmates alleged that Ohio officials denied them the right to ceremonial religious items and otherwise discriminated against them because of their religious beliefs. They claimed violations of the RLUIPA. The Ohio prison officials countered that the RLUIPA was unconstitutional because it advanced religion over nonreligion. They contended that such a law violated the Establishment Clause, which provides for separation between church and state. The Court ruled that the RLUIPA "qualifies as a permissible legislative accommodation of religion that is not barred by the Establishment Clause."[121]

The RLUIPA has led to greater religious freedom protection for inmates.

The RLUIPA has ensured that at least some inmates with meritorious claims obtain relief in the courts. For example, Colorado inmate Timothy Sheline sued the Colorado Department of Corrections after he was denied the right to a kosher meal, a requirement of his Orthodox Jewish faith. Sheline did not eat because he could not obtain kosher food, and as a result he suffered from a nearly 30-pound weight loss in prison. With legal help from the American Civil Liberties Union of Colorado, Sheline was able to get prison officials to restore his kosher diet.[122]

In 2006, a federal court in Oklahoma recognized that a Muslim inmate named Tyrone R. Hammons stated a claim under the RLUIPA when he alleged that prison officials denied him the right to purchase prayer oils that were central to his practice of Islam. The court recognized that Hammons's complaint indicated that prison restrictions "significantly modif[ied] his religious behavior and violat[ed] his beliefs by affecting his daily prayers."[123]

The RLUIPA ensures that inmates are treated with a certain level of respect and dignity. Attorney James D. Standish wrote, "RLUIPA is a step in the right direction of ensuring that this basic human dignity is afforded to the least among us. As such, it not only serves society's interest in providing opportunity for reform, but also ennobles the nation."[124]

Summary

Religious freedom is essential in prison. Inmates' mental well-being and chance for rehabilitation often depend on having a solid moral grounding. Religion provides that for millions of people in the world. More than any group of individuals in society, prisoners need protection from restrictions on religious liberty. The Bill of Rights in the U.S. Constitution was designed in large part to protect minorities, and no minority needs more protection than prisoners—people whose lives are under total control by government officials. Most noninmates can attend whatever church they want whenever they want. The spiritual lives of free citizens are totally under their control. Such is not the case for inmates, many of whom must remain in their cells for nearly the entire day with numerous restrictions. Attorney and legal commentator James Standish wrote that "prisoners are just the sort of unpopular minority the Bill of Rights was designed to protect."[125]

The U.S. Supreme Court has recognized that prisoners retain a First Amendment right to freely exercise their religious faith. When the Court created a standard that was not sufficiently protective of inmate rights to religious liberty, Congress passed a law that provided even more protection. This latest law—the RLUIPA—helps ensure that inmates retain their constitutional rights to freely exercise their religious faith behind bars.

Prisons Provide Sufficient Medical Care and Spend Enough for Inmates' Medical Needs

Oregon inmate Horacio Alberto Reyes-Camarena may receive a kidney transplant while he sits on death row. The state of Oregon pays more than $120,000 a year to keep Reyes-Camarena on dialysis, even though this man was convicted more than a decade ago of brutally stabbing two sisters, one of whom died. The surviving sister recovered from her 17 stab wounds to help prosecutors convict Reyes-Camarena and seek a death sentence. Reyes-Camarena may become the state's first death-row inmate to receive an organ transplant. "There's no doubt—there's no debate—that people have lost their lives while murderers have received transplants," says Dudley Sharp of the victims' rights group Justice for All.[126]

Sharp and others expressed outrage that a convicted murderer on death row might receive an organ transplant while more deserving, innocent potential recipients die while on a waiting list for organs. The Oregon State Department of Corrections denied Reyes-Camarena a kidney transplant, but not before setting off a national debate on the subject.[127]

As strange as it may sound, Reyes-Camarena's case is not an isolated one. Inmates in other states have sought organ transplants before.[128] For example, the state of California spent nearly $1 million to fund a heart transplant for an inmate.[129] A legislator in Louisiana became so upset over what happened in California that he introduced a bill in his own state house to prevent inmates from receiving expensive transplants.[130] The legislation sailed through both state legislative houses and was signed into law by the governor.

From the Louisiana Legislature

Medical care of inmates; testing

The secretary of public safety and corrections shall establish and shall prescribe standards for health, medical, and dental services for each institution, including preventive, diagnostic, and therapeutic measures on both an outpatient and a hospital basis, for all types of patients. An inmate may be taken to a medical facility outside the institution when deemed necessary by the director. However, in situations which are not life-threatening, the medical facility selected to treat the inmate shall be a part of the state's charity hospital system. No monies appropriated to the department from the state general fund or from dedicated funds shall be used for medical costs associated with organ transplants for inmates or for the purposes of providing cosmetic medical treatment of inmates, unless the condition necessitating such treatment or organ transplant arises or results from an accident or situation which was the fault of the department or resulted from an action or lack of action on the part of the department. However, nothing in this Section shall prohibit an inmate from donating his vital organs for transplant purposes.

Source: La. R.S. 15:831 (2006).

The U.S. Supreme Court established the proper standard of deliberate indifference with regard to prisoner medical care.

The U.S. Supreme Court provided a workable standard with respect to inmates' medical claims and needs in its 1976 decision *Estelle v. Gamble*.[131] The Court established that prison officials violate an inmate's constitutional right to medical care if they act with deliberate indifference. *Estelle* involved a Texas inmate named J.W. Gamble, who injured his back lifting a bale of cotton. Gamble reported to the prison infirmary, where he received some pain pills. Unfortunately, Gamble's pain continued, so he saw a doctor, who gave him a muscle relaxant. The prison doctor also said that Gamble should be given a cell pass, meaning he would not have to perform any work. Gamble continued to report pain in his back, but prison officials told him he had to return to work. When Gamble refused, the officials placed him in solitary confinement.[132] Several times prison officials refused to allow Gamble to see a doctor when he complained of back or chest pains.

Gamble sued, claiming that the officials subjected him to cruel and unusual punishment in violation of the Eighth Amendment. The U.S. Supreme Court determined that prison officials violated the Eighth Amendment when acting with deliberate indifference to the serious medical needs of inmates. "Regardless of how evidenced, deliberate indifference to a prisoner's serious illness or injury states a cause of action under Section 1983 [a federal civil rights statute]," Justice Thurgood Marshall wrote for the Court.[133] "This conclusion does not mean, however, that every claim by a prisoner that he has not received adequate medical treatment states a violation of the Eighth Amendment."[134]

This standard makes clear that mere negligence, or fault, does not make prison officials liable for every medical mistake made by the prison staff. In Gamble's case, he had alleged that prison officials violated his constitutional rights because they did not take X-rays or perform additional tests early in his treatment. "But the question whether an X-ray or additional

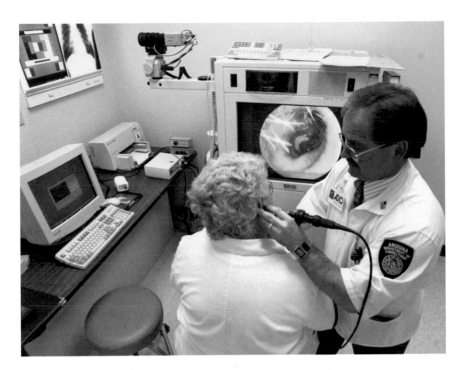

This new radiology transmission unit will allow prisoners to be evaluated for medical problems with a specialist looking at a large monitor at a separate medical center, so that inmates do not have to be transported to the doctor for a diagnosis. Health care for prisoners continues to be a controversial issue even as advances such as this are made.

techniques or forms of treatment is indicated is a classic example of a matter for medical judgment," the Court wrote.[135] In a later decision, the Court clarified that deliberate indifference means that "the official knows of and disregards an excessive risk to inmate health or safety."[136] Other courts have explained that the prison officials must have "(1) a subjective knowledge of a substantial risk of serious harm; (2) disregard of that risk; (3) and by conduct that is more than mere negligence."[137]

Lower courts have generally applied this "deliberate indifference" standard to reject most inmate claims under the Eighth Amendment for medical complaints. Take the case of Illinois inmate Brian Jones, who had a history of rectal bleeding. Prison medical staff determined that Jones's hemorrhoid problem required surgery, which they performed. Some of Jones's medical records were inaccurate as to the dates of prior surgeries and other details. Prison medical staff later performed two other surgeries on Jones before sending him to a specialist at the University of Illinois hospital in Chicago.

Jones contended that the lack of reliability of the medical records, failure to treat him, and the failure to treat him properly amounted to deliberate indifference. A federal district court in Illinois rejected Jones's claims in *Jones v. Natesha*.[138] Applying the deliberate indifference standard, the court found no constitutional fault on the part of the prison doctors. The court noted that prison doctors had seen Jones on 413 instances during his stay in the prison—an average of once every other day.[139] The court also noted that "evidence of differences of opinion as to whether one course of treatment is preferable to another is insufficient to state a constitutional claim under the Eighth Amendment."[140]

FROM THE BENCH

Estelle v. Gamble

Similarly, in the medical context, an inadvertent failure to provide adequate medical care cannot be said to constitute "an unnecessary and wanton infliction of pain" or to be "repugnant to the conscience of mankind." Thus, a complaint that a physician has been negligent in diagnosing or treating a medical condition does not state a valid claim of medical malpractice under the Eighth Amendment. Medical malpractice does not become a constitutional violation merely because the victim is a prisoner. In order to state a cognizable claim, a prisoner must allege acts or omissions sufficiently harmful to evidence deliberate indifference to serious medical needs. It is only such indifference that can offend evolving standards of decency in violation of the Eighth Amendment.

Source: *Estelle v. Gamble*, 429 U.S. 97, 105-106 (1976).

In another recent case, a Georgia inmate claimed an Eighth Amendment violation because prison officials discontinued his Tylenol 3 medication, caused him to miss some of his diabetic meals, failed to regularly check his vital signs and blood sugar levels, and denied him wheelchair assistance.[141] The court concluded that none of these allegations amounted to deliberate indifference. "The Court cannot conclude that the missed diabetic meals created a risk of serious harm to Plaintiff's health," the court wrote. "Even if Plaintiff did suffer dizziness, dry mouth, and stomach sickness on the days he did not receive his diabetic meal, these alleged symptoms are insufficient to warrant a finding of a substantial risk of serious harm—particularly because Plaintiff continued to receive his diabetic meals on a fairly regular basis."[142]

Prisoners are not entitled to state of the art medical care.

Prison health costs are exorbitant and often excessive. In 2006, Michigan spent $190 million on prison health care. West Virginia's annual expenditure for prisoner health care costs has risen the last seven years from $7 million to more than $20 million.[143] In 2006, the North Carolina Department of Corrections budgeted $156 million to provide for inmate health care.[144] The prison budgets are already strained almost to a breaking point. The last thing prisons need to worry about is whether prisoners receive state of the art medical care, expensive organ transplants, or cosmetic surgeries.

Legal commentator Carrie S. Frank wrote:

> Considering the rising cost of healthcare and the lack of accessibility to prescription medication and healthcare, it is reasonable to conclude that medically credible procedures that are also extremely sophisticated, cost prohibitive, and not widely available lie outside the realm of medical care required by *Estelle*."[145]

Wesley P. Shields

At a time when a single medical procedure can cost tens of thousands of dollars and state and local governments are straining to comply with their budgets, a standard that makes no allowance for possible financial burdens may no longer be practical. The government certainly cannot deny its prisoners necessary medical treatments, but the law must begin to recognize that state coffers are not an endless source of free health care for all inmates. If prisoners are able to pay for their medical treatment while in custody, they should be required to do so. The government should not be compelled to pay for what the prisoner could provide for himself.

Source: Wesley P. Shields, "Prisoner Health Care: Is It Proper to Charge Inmates for Health Services?" *Houston Law Review* 32 (1995): 271, 280.

Frank explained that "*Estelle* merely intended to provide prisoners with a guaranty of basic medical care and not state of the art medical care."[146] Certainly, inmates who can afford to pay for their own medical care should be forced to reimburse the state.

Several states in fact do just that. Attempting to alleviate their crushing financial burdens, they require inmates who can pay for a portion of their medical care to do so. Colorado, Texas, and Nevada are examples of states that have adopted measures such as this. For example, Colorado law requires inmates to make co-payments when they receive medical and dental care.

It is true that inmates should receive basic medical care. Prison officials should not allow inmates to beat each other to death, nor should officials deny prisoners the medicine they need. Society must realize that prison health care costs are crippling state budgets. Free citizens do not have a right to free medical care, and it is puzzling that an inmate might receive better health care than a free citizen. The other problem is that many inmates arrive at prisons with serious medical conditions. A significant percentage of the inmate population has drug problems, which correlates to higher medical costs.

From the Colorado State Legislature

Medical visits - charge to inmates - legislative declaration

(1)   (a) The general assembly hereby finds that the system of charging inmates a three-dollar copayment for certain medical services, but not for other services, is confusing to department personnel and, as a result, is inconsistently applied. Furthermore, the general assembly has determined that such a system does not effectively discourage inmates from seeking unnecessary medical services. The general assembly also finds that the lack of uniform and detailed department medical records renders a constructive analysis of the copayments assessed against inmates at those facilities virtually impossible.

(b) The general assembly therefore finds and determines that the department should establish consistent copayments for all medical, dental, and optometric services rendered to or on behalf of inmates and should require the facilities rendering such services to follow specified procedures, including the maintenance of detailed records regarding the assessment of copayments....

(3)   The department shall communicate the new mandatory copayment policy to every correctional facility that provides medical, dental, and optometric services to or on behalf of inmates to ensure that all department personnel consistently and regularly assess the required copayment for medical, dental, and optometric services.

(4)   The executive director shall promulgate rules related to medical, dental, and optometric service copayments, which rules shall address ... the following:

(a) The amount of the consistent copayment to be assessed against an inmate's account for medical services ...;

(b) The amount of the consistent copayment to be charged against an inmate's account for dental and optometric services ...;

(c) The detailed procedures that department personnel are to follow in assessing such copayments;

(d) The specific and exclusive bases upon which a copayment may be waived by department personnel;

(e) The information to be obtained by department personnel at the time of the inmate's medical, dental, or optometric visit on a standardized department form ...; and

(f) Disciplinary action to be taken against department personnel who fail to assess the copayment.

(5)   The department shall monitor the information ... to ensure that the copayments are being assessed consistently to all inmates.

Source: Colo. Rev. Stat. Ann. § 17-1-113.

Additionally, many inmates suffer from mental health problems, which further strains the budgets. A recent study by the U.S. Department of Justice found that more than half of all prison and jail inmates have mental health problems.[147] The state cannot possibly be responsible for paying for the mental health care of all these inmates. There is just not enough money to go around in this day of limited budgets.

Summary

Most prison officials do the best they can to provide for prisoners with basic medical needs. The U.S. Supreme Court has recognized that inmates do have a constitutional right to such care. The Court established a specific standard: denial of necessary medical services amounting to deliberate indifference or wanton infliction of pain violates the cruel and unusual punishment clause of the Eighth Amendment.

It is extremely difficult to prove deliberate indifference in a court of law, and for good reason. Just because an inmate does not receive ideal medical care, or the most state of the art care, or the most expensive care, this does not mean that prison officials have violated the inmate's constitutional rights. Medical malpractice does not equal an Eighth Amendment violation simply because the person is an inmate.

Medical costs are staggering and the problems of many inmates with complicated drug, physical health, and mental health histories are formidable. There are limits to the amount of funds that states can spend on prison health care.

Prison Officials Must Provide Better Health Care for Inmates

The California prison system has exploded in population during the past 25 years. Unfortunately, the growth in inmate population had not been matched with a corresponding growth in the medical services provided at prison facilities. Numerous deaths have occurred in the prisons as a result of inadequate health care. Testimony at a June 2005 evidentiary hearing in Federal court established that about 65 prisoners died each year in state prisons from grossly inadequate medical care.

Testimony in the case also revealed that 80 percent of the higher management positions in the state's prison health care services division were vacant. Federal district court judge Thelton Henderson, who presided over the case, wrote that this was "akin to having a professional baseball team with only a relief pitcher and no infielders."[148] Among his findings, Judge Henderson later reported in a detailed opinion:

Legal Definition: Receiver

A receiver is the person appointed by a judge to take charge of the property, business, etc., of another person, to run the business, collect the receivables, etc., with the purpose of fulfilling the objective for which such receivers are appointed.

Source: "Receiver," Legal-Explanations.com: Legal Explanations in Plain English, http://www .legal-explanations.com/definitions/receiver.htm (accessed January 4, 2007).

The CDCR [California Department of Corrections and Rehabilitation] sorely lacks sufficient qualified physicians to provide adequate patient care to prisoners.[149]

Indeed, the evidence from multiple sources establishes that medical care too often sinks below gross negligence to outright cruelty"[150]

Expert review of prisoner deaths in the CDCR shows repeated gross departures from even minimal standards of care.[151]

The evidence establishes beyond a doubt that the CDCR fails to provide competent nurses to fill the needs of the prison medical care system.[152]

The medical records in most CDCR prisons are either in a shambles or non-existent.[153]

The physical conditions in many CDCR clinics are completely inadequate for the provision of medical care.[154]

After the hearing, Judge Henderson had heard enough. He ordered that the state prison system be placed under the control of a receiver, who would issue reports and recommendations and correct the deplorable conditions at these state prisons. Henderson appointed Robert Sillen, the former director of Santa Clara Valley Health and Hospital System, to serve as the receiver.[155]

Many prison inmates receive grossly inadequate medical care.

Sadly, the plight of inmates in California state correctional institutions is not unique. Many inmates across the country face the prospect of being housed in prisons and jails with very poor health care facilities and support. Consider the plight of Missouri inmate Leland Hunley, who one day suffered a spider bite on his foot that swelled to the size of a quarter. He went to the prison infirmary, where a nurse applied a salve and wrapped Hunley's foot. The bite caused Hunley even more pain, so he

---

U.S. District Judge Thelton Henderson

On June 30, 2005, after six days of evidentiary hearings, this Court ruled from the bench that it would establish a Receivership to take control of the delivery of medical services to all California state prisoners confined by the California Department of Corrections and Rehabilitation....

By all accounts, the California prison medical care system is broken beyond repair. The harm already done in this case to California's prison inmate population could not be more grave, and the threat of future injury and death is virtually guaranteed in the absence of drastic action. The Court has given defendants every reasonable opportunity to bring its prison medical system up to constitutional standards, and it is beyond reasonable dispute that the State has failed. Indeed, it is an uncontested fact that, on average, an inmate in one of California's prisons needlessly dies every six to seven days due to constitutional deficiencies in the CDCR's medical delivery system. This statistic, awful as it is, barely provides a window into the waste of human life occurring behind California's prison walls due to the gross failures of the medical delivery system.

It is clear to the Court that this unconscionable degree of suffering and death is sure to continue if the system is not dramatically overhauled. Decades of neglecting medical care while vastly expanding the size of the prison system has led to a state of institutional paralysis. The prison system is unable to function effectively and suffers a lack of will with respect to prisoner medical care.

Source: *Plata v. Schwarzenegger*, No. C01-1351 (N.D. Cal.) (October 3, 2005).

went back to the infirmary, where the nurse changed the dressing. The infection deepened and Hunley's foot became a black scab showing bone. The condition worsened to the extent that the only possible solution was to amputate his leg.[156]

Timothy Oliff, an Alabama inmate, died from pneumonia and a stomach infection because prison officials failed to treat his cold and declined to take him to an outside hospital when his condition worsened. He was only 43 years old.[157] Another

FROM THE BENCH

Consent Decree in Mississippi Prison Conditions Case

Defendants shall ensure that the cell to which a prisoner is moved is clean prior to the move. Adequate cleaning supplies and equipment shall be provided in order that they may clean their cells at least weekly or more frequently as may be required to provide for basic sanitation and hygiene....

Defendants shall implement and maintain an effective mosquito eradication and pest control program....

Defendants shall comply, and shall ensure that their medical services provider complies, with the mandatory ACA Standards for Adult Correctional Institutions (4th Ed.) and with the essential National Commission on Correctional Healthcare (NCCHC) Standards for Health Care in Prison (2003); and shall be fully accredited by these organizations at all times. To effectuate the goals of this paragraph, Plaintiffs' expert will periodically audit the provision of care. Defendants will require their medical services provider to cooperate fully with these audits. Within 30 working days of the completion of the audit, Plaintiffs will furnish Defendants and their medical care provider with a report identifying deficiencies, if any. Within 45 days after receipt of that report, Defendants will submit a written plan to address any such deficiencies. In addition:

(a) Defendants shall ensure compliance with ACA Standard 4-4345 on medical co-payment fees;

(b) Defendants shall provide a chronic disease program that adequately identifies, monitors, and treats patients with chronic diseases, consistent with NCCHC Standard P-G-02 and ACA Standard 4-4359.

Source: Consent Decree in *Presley v. Epps,* No 4:05CV148-M-D, http://www.aclu.org/prison/conditions/27441lgl20060215.html (accessed January 5, 2007).

Alabama inmate, 28-year-old Pamela Brown, died suddenly in March 2001 after suffering from a heart condition, severe headaches, and blackouts. Reports showed that Brown had a "history of tightness of the chest during the last several months" and had previously collapsed a month before her death.[158] Yet prison officials failed to give her proper medical care.

Jeff Gerritt, an editorial writer for the *Detroit Free Press*, wrote a piece that exposed the unhealthy medical care in Michigan prisons.

> Court documents, medical records, and interviews with dozens of prisoners and their advocates show that incompetent and negligent medical care, misdiagnoses, delayed or denied treatment, withheld pain medication, and poor accommodations for people with disabilities are common in Michigan prisons—and have been for decades.[159]

Problems with health care in Michigan prisons caused Governor Jennifer Granholm in 2006 to order an independent review of the state's prison health care system.[160] Additionally, in December 2006, a federal judge issued an order threatening prison officials with a $2 million fine if they did not fill medical staff vacancies and improve health care in the state.[161]

In October 2002, the state of Washington had to pay $1 million to the family of a 32-year-old inmate who was denied access to a prison health clinic even though he was gravely ill and had been previously diagnosed with hepatitis C.[162] A class action lawsuit in Mississippi challenged the conditions of a super maximum security prison in Parchman, Mississippi. According to the complaint, "the severe lack of sanitation makes the prisoners extremely susceptible to drug-resistant staph infection (MRSA), a highly contagious bacteria that rapidly spreads in institutional settings through dirty laundry and unsanitized surfaces."[163] The complaint also alleged that the profound isolation and disgusting conditions at the prison created a situation in which many inmates developed mental illnesses.[164] In February 2006, the state agreed to enter into a consent decree agreeing to improve conditions at the Mississippi State Penitentiary.

Private, for-profit companies are more concerned with profit than adequate health care.

In the fictional HBO television series *OZ*, inmates in Oswald Correctional Facility began dying in part because the prison had contracted out their health care services to Weigert Corporation, a private company, which cut inmate medical benefits and treatments in order to save money. The Weigert Corporation in the TV series sacrificed inmate health on the altar of price. Though *OZ* and the Weigert Corporation are fictional creations, they are based at least in part on real life.

Many states have contracts with private, for-profit companies to provide health care for prisoners. The problem is that some of these companies appear to place the goal of profit above the Hippocratic Oath and good health. The *New York Times* reported that one such for-profit corporation, Prison Health Services, had won many jail contracts to provide health services. The problem was that "a yearlong examination of

New York Times writer Paul von Zielbauer

The examination of Prison Health also reveals a company that is very much a creature of a growing phenomenon, the privatization of jail and prison health care. As governments try to shed the burden of soaring medical costs—driven by the exploding problems of AIDS and mental illness among inmates—this field has become a $2 billion-a-year industry.

Source: Paul von Zielbauer, "As Health Care in Jails Goes Private, 10 Days Can Be a Death Sentence," *New York Times,* February 27, 2005.

Prison Health . . . reveals repeated instances of medical care that has been flawed and sometimes lethal."[165] According to the *Times*, Prison Health has "paid millions of dollars in fines and settlements."[166]

If inmates don't receive decent health care in prison, the rest of society will pay.

Many prison inmates will be released at some point. If these inmates do not receive decent health care while incarcerated, they may create a serious financial burden on the medical system when they are released. Additionally, many inmates with communicable diseases, particularly if these diseases are not treated in prison, will transmit those diseases to others when they are released. The health care problem in prisons is important given the sheer number of inmates who suffer from communicable diseases. A sizable percentage of the U.S. population infected with the AIDS virus is housed in prisons.

In a 2002 study entitled "The Health Status of Soon-To-Be-Released Inmates," the National Commission on Correctional Health Care warned:

> Inmates with communicable diseases who are released without having been effectively treated may transmit these conditions in the community, threatening public health.
>
> Inmates who are released with untreated conditions may become a serious financial burden on community health care systems.[167]

Inmates receive woefully deficient mental health care.

As bad as traditional health care in prison is, inmates receive even worse mental health treatment. A U.S. Department of Justice study released in September 2006 reports that more than half of all prison inmates have some type of mental health

The National Commission on Correctional Health Care Study (2002)

Few jails provide a comprehensive range of mental health services. Only 60 percent provide mental health evaluations, 42 percent provide psychiatric medications, 43 percent provide crisis intervention services, and 72 percent provide access to inpatient hospitalization. A majority of state adult prisons provide screening and assessment for mental illness, medication and medication monitoring, counseling or verbal therapy, and access to inpatient care. Only 36 percent of prisons have specialized housing for individuals with stable mental health conditions.

Continuity of care for inmates released with communicable disease, chronic disease, and mental illness is especially inadequate. Only 21 percent of jails provide case management or prerelease planning for mentally ill inmates.

Source: National Commission on Correctional Health Care, "The Health Status of Soon-To-Be Released Inmates" (March 2002).

problem.[168] Unfortunately, the study also determined that most inmates with mental health problems do not receive treatment for these disorders or ailments. The study reported that only 1 in 3 prison inmates and 1 in 6 jail inmates with mental health histories received treatment when they were incarcerated.[169]

Prison officials have a constitutional duty to provide some level of mental health services to their inmates. In *Bowring v. Godwin* (1977), the 4th U.S. Circuit Court of Appeals wrote:

> We see no underlying distinction between the right to medical care for physical ills and its psychological or psychiatric counterpart. Modern science has rejected the notion that mental or emotional disturbances are the products of afflicted souls, hence beyond the purview of counseling, medication, and therapy.[170]

Prisons are supposed to be in the business of rehabilitating inmates and preparing them at some point to return to society. Inmates with mental illnesses will not be able to return to society in a productive manner if they do not receive treatment for such illnesses.

Government officials, including prison administrators, should consider an alternative, structural approach to mental health care, which will help keep down the admittedly high costs of providing mental health treatment to some people in the criminal justice system. The Bazelon Center for Mental Health Law advocates for the creation of more "mental health courts," which can alleviate some of the burden on traditional jails.[171] The center explains.

FROM THE BENCH

Bowring v. Godwin

We therefore hold that Bowring (or any other prison inmate) is entitled to psychological or psychiatric treatment if a physician or other health care provider, exercising ordinary skill and care at the time of observation, concludes with reasonable medical certainty: (1) that the prisoner's symptoms evidence a serious disease or injury; (2) that such disease or injury is curable or may be substantially alleviated; and (3) that the potential for harm to the prisoner by reason of delay or the denial of care would be substantial. The right of treatment is, of course, limited to that which may be provided upon a reasonable cost and time basis and the essential test is one of medical necessity and not simply that which may be considered merely desirable.

This limited right to treatment stems from the Eighth Amendment, whose language must be interpreted in light of the evolving standards of decency that mark the progress of a maturing society. It is also premised upon notions of rehabilitation and the desire to render inmates useful and productive citizens upon their release.

Source: *Bowring v. Godwin*, 551 F.2d 44, 47-48 (4th Cir. 1977).

The goals of mental health courts, then, are: 1) to break the cycle of worsening mental illness and criminal behavior that begins with the failure of the community mental health system and is accelerated by the inadequacy of treatment in prisons and jails; and 2) to provide effective treatment options instead of the usual criminal sanctions for offenders with mental illnesses.[172]

Summary

Inmates must be provided with medical care for both physical and psychological illnesses. If the state is going to take away a person's liberty and confine him or her, it should at least provide adequate care for the duration. The U.S. Supreme Court has provided that deliberate indifference to serious inmate medical needs constitutes a violation of the Eighth Amendment. Many prisons and jails across the country are in a moment of crisis because they fail to provide adequate care. Too many prisons have contracted out with private companies that sacrifice inmate health in the name of expediency and cost efficiency.

Too many inmates are left with inadequate mental health services, as well. This presents a problem, as many inmates will reenter society with mental illnesses and other health problems. Prison administrators should follow the recommendations of groups such as the Bazelon Center for Mental Health Law and call for structural change, including the creation of mental health courts, which can alleviate some of the burdens on prisons and jails.

The Continuing Controversy over Inmate Rights

T he subject of prisoners' rights does not stop with the divisive issues of the Prison Litigation Reform Act, religious liberty and the Religious Land Use and Institutionalized Persons Act, and health care for prisoners. Numerous other prisoners' rights issues flood the courts and pervade the public consciousness.

The Problem of Prison Rape

One recent example concerns efforts to address the perennial problem of inmate violence. Some inmates are violent individuals who prey on other inmates. Some people are essentially sexual predators who obtain their gratification by imposing their will on weaker people.

The U.S. Supreme Court ruled that prison officials can be liable for violating an inmate's Eighth Amendment rights if they knowingly expose him to a substantial risk of sexual assault. In

Farmer v. Brennan (1994), the Court addressed a case involving a young transsexual in an all-male, maximum-security prison who alleged that he was raped and beaten only two weeks into his incarceration.[173] The Court determined that "a prison official may be held liable under the Eighth Amendment for denying humane conditions of confinement only if he knows that inmates face a substantial risk of serious harm and disregards that risk by failing to take reasonable measures to abate it."[174]

Congress entered into this debate and passed the Prison Rape Elimination Act of 2003.[175] The law essentially seeks to obtain detailed data about just how bad the problem is. Some of the findings Congress noted were that "at least 13 percent of the inmates in the United States have been sexually assaulted in prison."[176] Congress also noted that "juveniles are 5 times more likely to be sexually assaulted in adult rather than juvenile facilities—often within the first 48 hours of incarceration."[177]

FROM THE BENCH

Justice Harry Blackmun on *Farmer v. Brennan*

Homosexual rape or other violence among prison inmates serves absolutely no penological purpose. Such brutality is the equivalent of torture, and is offensive to any modern standard of human dignity. The horrors experienced by many young inmates, particularly those who, like petitioner, are convicted of nonviolent offenses, border on the unimaginable. Prison rape not only threatens the lives of those who fall prey to their aggressors, but is potentially devastating to the human spirit. Shame, depression, and a shattering loss of self-esteem accompany the perpetual terror the victim thereafter must endure. Unable to fend for himself without the protection of prison officials, the victim finds himself at the mercy of larger, stronger, and ruthless inmates. Although formally sentenced to a term of incarceration, many inmates discover that their punishment, even for nonviolent offenses like credit card fraud or tax evasion, degenerates into a reign of terror unmitigated by the protection supposedly afforded by prison officials.

Source: *Farmer v. Brennan,* 511 U.S. 825, 853 (J. Blackmun, concurring).

THE LETTER OF THE LAW

Legislative Language: Purposes of the Prison Rape Elimination Act of 2003

The purposes of this [Act] are to:

(1)   establish a zero-tolerance standard for the incidence of prison rape in prisons in the United States;

(2)   make the prevention of rape a top priority in each prison system;

(3)   develop and implement national standards for the detention, prevention, reduction, and punishment of prison rape;

(4)   increase the available data and information on the incidence of prison rape, consequently improving the management and administration of correctional facilities;

(5)   standardize the definitions used for collecting data on the incidence of prison rape;

(6)   increase the accountability of prison officials who fail to detect, prevent, reduce, and punish prison rape;

(7)   protect the Eighth Amendment rights of Federal, State, and local prisoners;

(8)   increase the efficiency and effectiveness of Federal expenditures through grant programs such as those dealing with health care; mental health care; disease prevention; crime prevention, investigation and prosecution; prison construction, maintenance, and operation; race relations; poverty; unemployment; and homelessness; and;

(9)   reduce the costs that prison rape imposes on interstate commerce.

Source: 42 U.S.C. § 15602.

Section 4 of the law requires the Bureau of Justice Statistics to conduct a "comprehensive statistical review and analysis" regarding the "incidence and effects of prison rape."[178] In July 2006, the Bureau of Justice Statistics fulfilled this task and produced a detailed report entitled "Sexual Violence Reported by Correctional Authorities, 2005." Among its findings were that there were 6,241 allegations of sexual violence in prison and jail reported in 2005 and that correctional authorities were able to verify 885 of those incidents.[179]

Nearly everyone agrees that rape is a problem in prisons, but questions remain as to how many sexual assaults go unreported. Inmates likely are reluctant to complain about sexual assaults, particularly by staff members, for fear of retaliation. Inmates also may feel great shame about the attacks and may not want to disclose information about them, lest they face the embarrassment that follows such a reporting. Suffice it to say, as more data is collected concerning prison rape, there likely will be further federal and state legislation on the subject.

The Problem of Mail Censorship

Another continuing problem concerns the censorship of prisoner mail. Prisoners often allege that prison officials retaliate against them by denying them access to their mail. For instance, a common complaint is that, after a prisoner files some sort of grievance, a prison guard will destroy or delay the receipt of the inmate's mail. Mail censorship was actually one of the complaints that led to the famous Attica prison uprising. Fast-forward 35 years later and complaints still abound in this sensitive area. As inmates have fewer rights with respect to visitation, the only contact many inmates have with the outside world is through letters, books, magazines, and the like. Supreme Court Justice Thurgood Marshall recognized this in 1974 when he wrote, "the mails provide one of the few ties inmates retain to their communities or families—ties essential to the success of their later return to the outside world."[180]

Prison officials contend that mail censorship is sometimes necessary because prisoners may receive contraband or information to plan escapes through the mail. They also sometimes receive highly inflammatory material through the mail that could, for instance, be used to incite racial tensions. Many important U.S. Supreme Court decisions involved restrictions on inmate mail. In *Procunier v. Martinez* (1974), the high court addressed mail restrictions instituted by the California Department of Corrections.[181] In *Martinez,* the high court struck down a California prison regulation prohibiting correspondence between inmates and noninmates that "unduly complain," "magnify grievances," or "express inflammatory political, racial, religious or other views or beliefs." The Court determined this was

FROM THE BENCH

Justice Thurgood Marshall on *Procunier v. Martinez*

First Amendment guarantees protect the free and uninterrupted interchange of ideas upon which a democratic society thrives. Perhaps the most obvious victim of the indirect censorship effected by a policy of allowing prison authorities to read inmate mail is criticism of prison administration. The threat of identification and reprisal inherent in allowing correctional authorities to read prisoner mail is not lost on inmates who might otherwise criticize their jailers. The mails are one of the few vehicles prisoners have for informing the community about their existence and, in these days of strife in our correctional institutions, the plight of prisoners is a matter of urgent public concern. To sustain a policy which chills the communication necessary to inform the public on this issue is at odds with the most basic tenets of the guarantee of freedom of speech.

The First Amendment serves not only the needs of the polity but also those of the human spirit—a spirit that demands self-expression. Such expression is an integral part of the development of ideas and a sense of identity. To suppress expression is to reject the basic human desire for recognition and affront the individual's worth and dignity. Such restraint may be "the greatest displeasure and indignity to a free and knowing spirit that can be put upon him." When the prison gates slam behind an inmate, he does not lose his human quality; his mind does not become closed to ideas; his intellect does not cease to feed on a free and open interchange of opinions; his yearning for self-respect does not end; nor is his quest for self-realization concluded. If anything, the needs for identity and self-respect are more compelling in the dehumanizing prison environment. Whether an O. Henry writing his short stories in a jail cell or a frightened young inmate writing his family, a prisoner needs a medium for self-expression. It is the role of the First Amendment and this Court to protect those precious personal rights by which we satisfy such basic yearnings of the human spirit.

Source: *Procunier v. Martinez*, 416 U.S. 396, 427 (J. Marshall, concurring).

unconstitutional because the regulations were broader than the security interests of the prison. The high court based its ruling in part on the First Amendment rights of the noninmates.

The aforementioned *Turner v. Safley* decision involved in part a Missouri Department of Corrections policy that prohibited inmates from sending and receiving mail from other inmates.[182] In *Thornburgh v. Abbott* (1989), the U.S. Supreme Court upheld a Federal Bureau of Prisons rule that enabled wardens to restrict inmate mail "only if it is determined detrimental to the security, good order, or discipline of the institution or if it might facilitate criminal activity." In *Thornburgh*, the Supreme Court determined that the *Martinez* case should be "limited to regulations concerning outgoing correspondence," noting that "[the] implications of outgoing correspondence for prison security are of a categorically lesser magnitude than the implications of incoming materials."[183]

One current aspect of this issue concerns restrictions on inmates receiving materials that were generated from the Internet. Prison officials have argued that material from the Internet poses special security risks because it is easier to send coded messages in e-mails, and because it is easier for people to remain anonymous when sending Internet-generated material. Both a federal district court and a federal appeals court in California rejected the contentions of the prison officials and determined that the ban on inmates receiving Internet-generated mail was unreasonable. The appeals court noted that "the California Department of Corrections did not support its assertion that coded messages are more likely to be inserted into Internet-generated materials than word-processed documents."[184] The court also pointed out that "prohibiting all Internet-generated mail is an arbitrary way to achieve a reduction in mail volume."[185] One legal commentator wrote, "blanket prohibitions of inmate Internet access via indirect means would open the flood gates, allowing for various types of speech to be censored even outside the prison arena."[186]

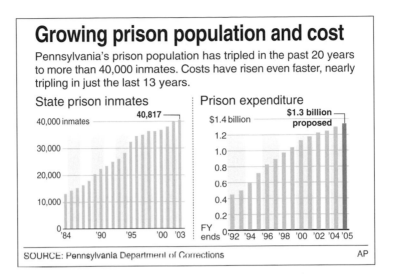

Growing prison population and cost

Pennsylvania's prison population has tripled in the past 20 years to more than 40,000 inmates. Costs have risen even faster, nearly tripling in just the last 13 years.

State prison inmates

40,000 inmates — 40,817

30,000

20,000

10,000

0
'84   '90   '95   '00 '03

Prison expenditure

$1.4 billion — $1.3 billion proposed

1.2
1.0
0.8
0.6
0.4
0.2
FY 0
ends '92 '94 '96 '98 '00 '02 '04 '05

SOURCE: Pennsylvania Department of Corrections   AP

The charts above show the number of prison inmates in Pennsylvania and prison expenditures over the years. As costs continue to rise, issues of prison reform will continue to be debated into the future.

Still another area involving censorship of mail concerns pornography in prisons. The federal courts have upheld many restrictions on pornography, citing testimony from prison officials that the measures are helpful for rehabilitative purposes and the prevention of sexual assaults. The United States Court of Appeals for the District of Columbia upheld a prison policy that banned pornographic magazines for inmates. "We think that the government could rationally have seen a connection between pornography and rehabilitative values." The court determined that the idea that excluding pornography will rehabilitate prisoners "may be optimistic, but it is not irrational." The court majority added: "Common sense tells us that prisoners are more likely to develop the now-missing self-control and respect for others if prevented from poring over pictures that are themselves degrading and disrespectful."[187]

The debates over inmate violence and various restrictions on inmates' reading materials show that constitutional conflicts often arise behind prison walls. These conflicts arouse the anger of people who believe that inmate suits are frivolous, waste government resources, and drain public funds. Many people believe that the federal courts are clogged with too many prisoner lawsuits. Congress heeded some of these concerns by passing the Prison Litigation Reform Act, designed to weed out frivolous inmate claims.

Because prisoners are under the constant supervision of government officials, however, some critics counter that prisoners are most in need of judicial review to protect the constitutional freedoms they still possess. The Bill of Rights was designed to protect those in the minority and those most in need of protection. Supreme Court Justice Felix Frankfurter said it eloquently: "It is a fair summary of history to say that the safeguards of liberty have frequently been forged in controversies involving not very nice people."[188]

Prisoners' lawsuits highlight issues that otherwise might not garner attention from the general public. Many people would just as soon forget about prison conditions and how they affect inmates—instead, they simply urge the construction of more prisons in order to solve problems such as overcrowding. Other people contend that society should address the treatment of prisoners because many of them will one day return to our communities, and they should be given the tools to integrate back into society as seamlessly as possible. Finally, many people believe that how we treat marginalized populations is a crucial measure of a humane and enlightened society.

NOTES

Introduction: Prisoners' Rights

1 Winston Churchill, Parliamentary speech on July 20, 1910, quoted in David L. Hudson, Jr., "Why Two Federal Appeals Courts Were Right to Strike Down Limitations on Inmate Visits—One of Which Unfairly Targeted Gay Inmates," Findlaw.com, September 12, 2002, http://writ.news.findlaw.com/commentary/20020912_hudson.html (accessed January 4, 2007).

2 *Turner v. Safley*, 482 U.S. 78, 84 (1987).

3 *Ruffin v. Commonwealth*, 62 Va. 790 (1871).

4 Hedieh Nasheri, "A Spirit of Meanness: Courts, Prisons and Prisoners," *Cumberland Law Review* 27 (1996): 1173, 1175–1176.

5 Ibid., 1177.

6 *Lee v. Washington*, 390 U.S. 333 (1968).

7 *Procunier v. Martinez*, 416 U.S. 396 (1974).

8 378 U.S. 546 (1964).

9 393 U.S. 493 (1969).

10 *Cruz v. Beto*, 405 U.S. 319 (1972).

11 Talking History, "Attica Revisited," http://www.talkinghistory.org/attica/index.html (accessed January 4, 2007).

12 Bruce Jackson, "Attica: An Anniversary of Death," *Artvoice*, September 9, 1999, http://www.acsu.buffalo.edu/~bjackson/attica.htm (accessed January 4, 2007).

13 Jessica Feierman, "Pro Se Litigation Ten Years After AEDPA: 'The Power of the Pen': Jailhouse Lawyers, Literacy, and Civic Engagement," *Harvard Civil Rights-Civil Liberties Law Review* 41 (2006): 369, 370.

14 *Trop v. Dulles*, 356 U.S. 86, 101 (1958).

15 365 U.S. 167 (1961).

16 404 F.2d 571 (8th Cir. 1968).

17 *Hudson v. McMillan*, 503 U.S. 1, 9 (1992).

18 *Hope v. Pelzer*, 536 U.S. 730 (2002).

19 Nasheri, 1175.

20 *Turner v. Safley*, 482 U.S.

21 Ibid. at 89.

22 Ibid. at 90.

23 Ibid.

24 Ibid.

25 *Shaw v. Murphy*, 532 U.S. 223 (2001).

26 *Overton v. Bazzetta*, 539 U.S. 126 (2003).

27 *Beard v. Banks*, U.S. 126 S.Ct. 2572 (2006).

Point: It Is Reasonable to Place Limits on Prisoner Lawsuits

28 *McCleary v. Texas Department of Criminal Justice*, No. 14-98-01265-CV (Tex. App.) (May 17, 2001).

29 *Bailey v. Clemmons*, No. 05-963 (W.D. Pa.) (September 16, 2005).

30 *Anderson v. Pitcher*, No. 94-1254 (6th Cir.) (September 28, 1994).

31 41 Cong. Rec. S14413, September 27, 2005, http://frwebgate.access.gpo.gov/cgi-bin/getpage.cgi?dbname=1995_recor d&position=all&page=S14413 (accessed January 5, 2007).

32 Eugene J. Kuzinski, "The End of the Prison Law Firm? Frivolous Inmate Litigation, Judicial Oversight, and the Prison Litigation Reform Act of 1995," *Rutgers Law Journal* 29 (1998): 361, 366.

33 Brian J. Ostrom, Roger A. Hanson, and Fred L. Cheesman, II, "Congress, Courts and Corrections: An Empirical Perspective on the Prison Litigation Reform Act," *Notre Dame L. Rev.* 78 (2003): 527.

34 Peter Hobart, "The Prison Litigation Reform Act: Striking the Balance Between Law and Order," *Vill. L. Rev.* 44 (1999): 981.

35 Ibid., 362.

36 Ibid., 364.

37 141 Cong. Rec. S14413, September 27, 2005.

38 42 U.S.C. § 1997(e).

39 141 Cong. Rec. 14626, September 29, 2005, http://frwebgate2.access.gpo.gov/cgi-bin/waisgate.cgi?WAISdocID=38685 7303917+0+0+0&WAISaction=retrieve (accessed January 5, 2007).

40 John Scalia, "Prisoner Petitions Filed in U.S. District Courts, 2000, with Trends 1980–2000," Bureau of Justice Statistics Special Report, January 2002,

http://www.ojp.usdoj.gov/bjs/pub/pdf/
ppfusd00.pdf (accessed January 5, 2007).

41 Ostrom, Hanson, and Cheesman, 1525, 1585.

42 141 Cong. Rec. 14414, September 27, 2005.

43 Kuzinski, 369.

44 Ibid., 373.

45 18 U.S.C. § 3626(a)(1)(A).

46 530 U.S. 327 (2000).

47 Ibid. at 348.

48 Ibid. at 350.

49 28 U.S.C. § 1915(b)(1).

50 18 U.S.C. § 1915(b)(4).

51 *Heard v. Wetherington*, CV 602-107 (S.D. Ga.) (February 17, 2003).

52 *Green v. Camper*, 477 F.Supp. 758 (W.D. Mo. 1979).

53 Ibid. at 769.

Counterpoint: The PLRA Deprives Inmates of Access to the Courts and Represents an Unconstitutional Power Grab by Congress

54 *Porter v. Nussle*, 534 U.S. 516, 520-522 (2002).

55 42 U.S.C. § 1997e.

56 534 U.S., at 532.

57 American Civil Liberties Union, "The Top Ten Non-Frivolous Lawsuits Filed By Prisoners," *The Other Side of the Wall*, February 1996, http://www.prisonwall.org/ten.htm (accessed January 5, 2007).

58 Jon O. Newman, "A Jarring Loss," Letters to the Editor, *Newseek*, January 29, 1996, p. 16.

59 Jennifer Winslow, "The Prison Litigation Reform Act's Physical Injury Requirement Bars Meritorious Lawsuits: Was It Meant To?" *UCLA Law Review* 49 (2002): 1655, 1666.

60 42 U.S.C. § 1997e(a).

61 42 U.S.C. § 1997e(c)(1).

62 42 U.S.C. § 1997e(e).

63 Deborah M. Golden, "The Prison Litigation Reform Act: A Proposal for Closing the Loophole for Rapists," American Constitution Society for Law and Policy

(June 2006): 2, http://www.spr.org/pdf/The%20Prison%20Litigation%20Reform%20Act%20-A%20Proposal.pdf (accessed January 5, 2007).

64 Ibid., 7.

65 Barbara Belbot, "Report on the Prison Litigation Reform Act: What Have the Courts Decided So Far," *The Prison Journal* 84 (September 2004): 290, 296.

66 28 U.S.C. § 1915(b)(2).

67 28 U.S.C. § 1915(g).

68 *Rhodes v. Chapman*, 452 U.S. 337, 354 (1981) (J. Brennan, concurring).

69 18 U.S.C. § 3626(a)(1)(A).

70 18 U.S.C. § 3626(a)(2).

71 18 U.S.C. § 3626(e)(2).

72 Donna Lennon, "Reforming Prison Reform," Findlaw.com, http://writ.news.findlaw.com/commentary/20000808_lennon.html (accessed January 5, 2007).

73 Ibid.

74 *Hope v. Pelzer*, 536 U.S. 730 (2002).

75 *Rodriguez v. McClenning*, 399 F.Supp.2d 228 (S.D.N.Y. 2005).

76 Ibid. at 238.

Point: Inmates Have Adequate Constitutional Protection for Religious Liberty

77 James E. Robertson, "The Jurisprudence of the PLRA: Inmates as 'Outsiders' and the Countermajoritarian Difficulty," *Journal of Criminal Law and Criminology* 92 (2002): 187, 209.

78 *Theriault v. Silber*, 453 F.Supp. 254, 260 (W.D. Tex. 1978).

79 Ibid.

80 *Ochs v. Thalacker*, 90 F.3d 293, 296 (8th Cir. 1996).

81 Ibid.

82 *Saleem v. Helman*, No. 96-2502 (7th Cir.) (August 21, 1997).

83 482 U.S. 342 (1987).

84 Ibid. at 351.

85 Ibid. at 352.

86 42 U.S.C. § 2000bb.

87 42 U.S.C. § 2000cc.

88 *City of Boerne v. Flores*, 521 U.S. 507 (1997).

89 Marci Hamilton, "The Supreme Court's New Ruling on the Religious Land Use and Institutionalized Persons Act's Prison Provisions: Deferring Key Constitutional Questions," *Findlaw.com*, http://writ.news.findlaw.com/hamilton/20050602.html, (accessed January 5, 2007).

90 Morgan F. Johnson, "Heaven Help Us: The Religious Land Use and Institutionalized Persons Act's Prisoners Provisions in the Aftermath of the Supreme Court's Decision in Cutter v. Wilkinson," *American University Journal of Gender, Social Policy and the Law* 14 (2006): 585, 600.

91 *Cutter v. Wilkinson,* 349 F.3d 257, 266 (6th Cir. 2003).

92 544 U.S. 709 (2005).

93 Ibid. at 720.

94 544 U.S. at 721.

95 Ibid. at 722.

96 Ibid. at 723.

97 Johnson, 599.

98 *Cutter,* 544 U.S. at 726.

99 John W. Popeo, "Combating Radical Islam in Prisons Within the Legal Dictates of the Free Exercise Clause," *New England Journal on Criminal and Civil Confinement* 32 (2006): 135, 138.

100 Charles Colson, "What's Hidden in the Shadows: Radical Islam and U.S. Prisons," Breakpoint Commentaries, http://www.breakpoint.org/listingarticle.asp?ID=5628 (accessed January 5, 2007).

101 Popeo, 158.

102 Ibid.

Counterpoint: Inmates' Religious-liberty Rights Are Fundamental and Must Be Protected

103 *Warsoldier v. Wooford,* 418 F.3d 989 (9th Cir. 2005).

104 Ibid. at 992.

105 Ibid. at 997.

106 Ibid. at 999.

107 Ibid. at 1000.

108 Ibid.

109 Bob Greene, "Colson Conversion: From Preying to Praying," *Los Angeles Times,* April 4, 1976, F1.

110 Prison Fellowship Ministries, "About Chuck Colson," http://www.prisonfellowship.org/Bio.asp?ID=43 (accessed January 5, 2007).

111 James D. Standish, "Freedom Behind Bars," *Liberty* (September/October 2003): 3.

112 *Cooper v. Pate,* 324 F.2d 165 (7th Cir. 1963).

113 *Cooper v. Pate,* 378 U.S. 546 (1964).

114 *Cruz v. Beto,* 405 U.S. 319 (1972).

115 482 U.S. 78 (1987).

116 482 U.S. 342 (1987).

117 Shabazz, 482 U.S. at 349.

118 494 U.S. 872 (1990).

119 Senators Orrin Hatch and Edward Kennedy, joint statement,146 Congressional Record S7775, July 27, 2000.

120 544 U.S. 709 (2005).

121 Ibid. at 720.

122 ACLU of Colorado, "After ACLU Lawsuit, Colorado DOC Agrees to Restore Jewish Prisoner's Kosher Diet," http://www.aclu-co.org/news/pressrelease/release_kosher101305.htm (accessed January 5, 2007).

123 *Hammons v. Jones,* No. 00-CV-0143-CVE-SAJ (N.D. Okl.) (February 14, 2006).

124 Standish, 7.

125 Ibid.

Point: Prisons Provide Sufficient Medical Care and Spend Enough for Inmates' Medical Needs

126 Quoted in Bryan Robinson, "Death-Row Inmate Seeks Organ Transplant," ABC.news.com, http://abcnews.go.com/US/print?id=90611 (accessed January 5, 2007).

127 "State Rejects Transplant for Death Row Inmate," *Los Angeles Times,* June 17, 2003, 16.

128 Mark Andersen, "York Inmate Strives to Join Transplant List," *Lincoln Journal Star,* February 5, 2003, A1.

129 Carrie S. Frank, "Must Inmates Be Provided Free Organ Transplants?: Revisiting the Deliberate Indifference

Standard," *George Mason University Civil Rights Law Journal* 15 (2005): 341, 342.

130 Melinda DeSlatte, "House: Louisiana Shouldn't Pay for Transplants for Some Prisoners," *Associated Press*, June 5, 2003.

131 429 U.S. 97 (1976).

132 Ibid. at 100–101.

133 Ibid. at 105.

134 Ibid.

135 Ibid.at 107.

136 *Farmer v. Brennan*, 511 U.S. 825, 837 (1994).

137 *Gardner v. Ramsey*, 5:04-CV-121 (M.D. Ga.) (March 21, 2006).

138 233 F.Supp. 2d 1022 (N.D. Ill. 2002).

139 Ibid.at 1028.

140 Ibid.at 1029.

141 *Gardner v. Ramsey*, 5:04-CV-121.

142 Ibid.at *15.

143 "W.Va. Prisons Deal with Rising Medical Costs," *The Associated Press*, July 26, 2006.

144 "Health Care Costs on the Rise in U.s. Prisons," *Corrections Professional*, May 26, 2006.

145 Frank, 361.

146 Ibid., 368.

147 Department of Justice Press Release, "Study Finds More Than Half of All Prison and Jail Inmates Have Mental Health Problems," September 6, 2006, http://www.ojp.usdoj.gov/bjs/pub/press/mhppjipr.htm (accessed January 5, 2007).

Counterpoint: Prison Officials Must Provide Better Health Care for Inmates

148 *Plata v. Schwarzenegger*, No. C01-1351 (N.D. Cal.) (10/3/2005), at *14.

149 Ibid. at *15.

150 Ibid. at *16.

151 Ibid. at *20.

152 Ibid. at *27.

153 Ibid. at *39.

154 Ibid. at *41.

155 Josh Richman, "Reforms a Start in Con-trolling Prison Health Care Costs," *Contra Costa Times*, December 6, 2006, F4.

156 Joseph Url, "Michigan Prisons' Medical Care: A Reflection on the Obligations Owed to the Least Among Us," *Wayne Law Review* 51 (2005): 487, 487–488.

157 Sam Hodges, "Inmate Deaths: A Fact of Life," *Mobile Register*, May 11, 2003.

158 Ibid.

159 Jeff Gerritt, "Unhealthy Confinement: Inmates Aren't the Only Ones Who Pay for Poor Medical Care in Prison," *Detroit Free Press*, November 25, 2006, http://www.freep.com/apps/pbcs.dll/article?AID=/20060821/OPINION02/111250006/1068/OPINION (accessed January 5, 2007).

160 Jeff Gerritt, "Granholm Orders Review of Prison Health Care System; Move Follows Probe of Death, Longtime Troubles," *Detroit Free Press*, August 22, 2006, 1.

161 *Haddix v. Caruso*, No. 4:92-CV-110 (W.D. Mich.) (December 7, 2006), http://www.aclu.org/images/asset_upload_file904_27644.pdf (accessed January 5, 2007).

162 Angela Galloway, "Prison Death Costs State $1 Million: Lawsuit Alleging Shoddy Health Care, Rights Violations is Settled," *Seattle Post Intelligencer*, October 30, 2002, A1.

163 *Presley v. Epps*, No. 4:05CV148-M-B (N.D. Miss.) (filed June 22, 2005), http://www.aclu.org/prison/gen/14745lgl20050622.html (accessed January 5, 2007).

164 Ibid.

165 Paul von Zielbauer, "As Health Care in Jails Goes Private, 10 Days Can Be a Death Sentence," *New York Times*, February 27, 2005, http://www.nytimes.com/2005/02/27/nyregion/27jail.html?ex=1267333200&en=4b321a2e26a4f1d4&ei=5088&partner=rssnyt (accessed January 5, 2007).

166 Ibid.

167 National Commission on Correctional Health Care, "The Health Status of Soon-To-Be Released Inmates" (March

2002): ix, http://www.ncchc.org/pubs/pubs_stbr.html (accessed January 5, 2007).

168 Department of Justice, "Study Finds More Than Half of All Prison and Jail Inmates Have Mental Health Problems."

169 Doris J. James and Lauren E. Glaze, "Mental Health Problems of Prison and Jail Inmates," U.S. Department of Justice (September 2006): 1 http://www.ojp.usdoj.gov/bjs/abstract/mhppji.htm (accessed January 5, 2007).

170 551 F.2d 44, 47 (5th Cir. 1977).

171 Robert Bernstein and Tammy Seltzer, "The Role of Mental Health Courts in System Reform," The Bazelon Center for Mental Health Law, http://www.bazelon.org/issues/criminalization/publications/mentalhealthcourts/index.htm#intro (accessed January 5, 2007).

172 Ibid.

Conclusion: The Continuing Controversy over Inmate Rights

173 511 U.S. 825 (1994).

174 Ibid. at 847.

175 42 U.S.C. § 15601 et seq.

176 42 U.S.C. § 15601(2).

177 42 U.S.C. § 15601(4).

178 42 U.S.C. § 15603(a)(1).

179 Allen J. Beck and Paige M. Harrison, "Sexual Violence Reported by Correctional Authorities, 2005," Bureau of Justice Statistics Special Report (July 2006): 1, http://www.ojp.usdoj.gov/bjs/pub/pdf/svrca05.pdf (accessed January 5, 2007).

180 *Procunier v. Martinez*, 416 U.S. 396, 426 (J. Marshall, concurring).

181 416 U.S. 396 (1974).

182 482 U.S. 79 (1987).

183 490 U.S. 401 (1989).

184 *Clement v. California Department of Corrections*, 364 F.3d 1148, 1152 (9th Cir. 2004).

185 Ibid.

186 Titia A. Holtz, "Reaching Out From Behind Bars: The Constitutionality of Laws Barring Prisoners from the Internet," *Brooklyn Law Review* 67 (2002): 855, 898.

187 *Amatel v. Reno*, 156 F.3d 192 (D.C. Cir. 1998)

188 *U.S. v. Rabinowitz*, 339 U.S. 56, 69 (J. Frankfurter, dissenting).

Books and Articles

Beck, Allen J., and Paige M. Harrison. "Sexual Violence Reported by Correctional Authorities, 2005." Bureau of Justice Statistics Special Report. July 2006. Available online. URL: http://www.ojp.usdoj.gov/bjs/pub/pdf/svrca05.pdf. Accessed January 4, 2007.

Belbot, Barbara. "Report on the Prison Litigation Reform Act: What Have the Courts Decided So Far?" *The Prison Journal* 84 (September 2004): 290.

Colson, Charles. "What's Hidden in the Shadows: Radical Islam and U.S. Prisons." *Breakpoint Commentaries*, September 26, 2006. Available online. URL: http://www.breakpoint.org/listingarticle.asp?ID=5628. Accessed January 4, 2007.

Feierman, Jessica. "Pro Se Litigation Ten Years After AEDPA: 'The Power of the Pen': Jailhouse Lawyers, Literacy, and Civic Engagement." *Harvard Civil Rights-Civil Liberties Law Review* 41 (2006): 369.

Frank, Carrie S. "Must Inmates Be Provided Free Organ Transplants?: Revisiting the Deliberate Indifference Standard." *George Mason University Civil Rights Law Journal* 15 (2005): 341.

Gerritt, Jeff. "Unhealthy Confinement: Inmates Aren't the Only Ones Who Pay for Poor Medical Care in Prison." *Detroit Free Press*, November 25, 2006. Available online. URL: http://www.freep.com/apps/pbcs.dll/article?AID=/20060821/OPINION02/111250006/1068/OPINION. Accessed January 4, 2007.

Golden, Deborah M. "The Prison Litigation Reform Act: A Proposal for Closing the Loophole for Rapists." American Constitution Society for Law and Policy, June 2006. Available online. URL: http://www.spr.org/pdf/The%20Prison%20Litigation%20Reform%20Act%20A%20Proposal.pdf. Accessed January 4, 2007.

Hamilton, Marci. "The Supreme Court's New Ruling on the Religious Land Use and Institutionalized Persons Act's Prison Provisions: Deferring Key Constitutional Questions." Findlaw.com, June 2, 2005. Available online. URL: http:///writ.news.findlaw.com/hamilton/20050602.html.

Hobart, Peter. "The Prison Litigation Reform Act: Striking the Balance Between Law and Order." *Vill. L. Rev.* 44 (1999): 981.

Holtz, Titia A. "Reaching Out From Behind Bars: The Constitutionality of Laws Barring Prisoners from the Internet." *Brooklyn Law Review* 67 (2002): 855.

James, Doris J., and Lauren E. Glaze, "Mental Health Problems of Prison and Jail Inmates." U.S. Department of Justice, September 2006. Available online. URL: http://www.ojp.usdoj.gov/bjs/abstract/mhppji.htm. Accessed January 4, 2007.

Johnson, Calvin C.. and Greg Hampikian. *Exit to Freedom*. Athens, Ga.: University of Georgia Press, 2003.

Johnson, Morgan F. "Heaven Help Us: The Religious Land Use and Institutionalized Persons Act's Prisoners Provisions in the Aftermath of the Supreme Court's Decision in Cutter v. Wilkinson." *American University Journal of Gender, Social Policy & the Law* 14 (2006): 585.

Kuzinski, Eugene J. "The End of the Prison Law Firm? Frivolous Inmate Litigation, Judicial Oversight, and the Prison Litigation Reform Act of 1995." *Rutgers Law Journal* 29 (1998): 361.

Lennon, Donna. "Reforming Prison Reform." Findlaw.com, August 8, 2000. Available online. URL: http://writ.news.findlaw.com/commentary/20000808_lennon.html. Accessed January 4, 2007.

Lerner, Jimmy. *You Got Nothing Coming: Notes From a Prison Fish*. New York: Broadway Books, 2002.

Nasheri, Hedieh. "A Spirit of Meanness: Courts, Prisons and Prisoners." *Cumberland Law Review* 27 (1996): 1173.

National Commission on Correctional Health Care. "The Health Status of Soon-To-Be Released Inmates." March 2002. Available online. URL: http://www.ncchc.org/pubs/pubs_stbr.html. Accessed January 4, 2007.

Oshinsky, David J. *Worse Than Slavery: Parchman Farm and the Ordeal of Jim Crow Justice*. New York: The Free Press, 1996.

Ostrom, Brian J., Roger A. Hanson, and Fred L. Cheesman, II. "Congress, Courts and Corrections: An Empirical Perspective on the Prison Litigation Reform Act." *Notre Dame L. Rev.* 78 (2003): 1525.

Popeo, John W. "Combating Radical Islam in Prisons Within the Legal Dictates of the Free Exercise Clause." *New England Journal on Criminal and Civil Confinement* 32 (2006): 135.

Robertson, James E. "The Jurisprudence of the PLRA: Inmates as 'Outsiders' and the Countermajoritarian Difficulty." *Journal of Criminal Law & Criminology* 92 (2002): 187.

Santos, Michael G. *Inside: Life Behind Bars in America*. New York: St. Martin's Press, 2006.

Scalia, John. "Prisoner Petitions Filed in U.S. District Courts, 2000, with Trends 1980– 2000." Bureau of Justice Statistics Special Report, January 2002. Available online. URL: http://www.ojp.usdoj.gov/bjs/pub/pdf/ppfusd00.pdf. Accessed January 4, 2007.

RESOURCES ///////

Standish, James D. "Freedom Behind Bars." *Liberty* (September/October 2003).

Url, Joseph. "Michigan Prisons' Medical Care: A Reflection on the Obligations Owed to the Least Among Us." *Wayne Law Review* 51 (2005): 487.

von Zielbauer, Paul. "As Health Care in Jails Goes Private, 10 Days Can Be a Death Sentence." *New York Times*, February 27, 2005. Available online. URL: http://www.nytimes.com/2005/02/27/nyregion/27jail.html?ex=12 67333200&en=4b321a2e26a4f1d4&ei=5088&partner=rssnyt. Accessed January 4, 2007.

Winslow, Jennifer. "The Prison Litigation Reform Act's Physical Injury Requirement Bars Meritorious Lawsuits: Was It Meant To?" *UCLA Law Review* 49 (2002): 1655.

Web Sites

American Civil Liberties Union's National Prison Project
http://www.aclu.org/prison/index.html
The ACLU's Prison Project is a national litigation program on behalf of prisoners, primarily organized to fight unconstitutional conditions in prison.

Bureau of Justice Statistics
http://www.ojp.usdoj.gov/bjs
Provides statistics gathered by the Bureau of Justice, including information on crimes, victims, criminals, and the justice system.

Correctional Association of New York
http://www.correctionalassociation.org
The Correctional Association of New York is an independent, nonprofit organization given authority by the New York State Legislature to inspect prisons and to report its findings and recommendations to the legislature, the public, and the press.

Critical Resistance
http://www.criticalresistance.org
As a national grassroots group that fights to end the "prison industrial complex," Critical Resistance suggests alternatives to policing and prisons in order to keep communities safe.

Human Rights Watch on Prisons
http://hrw.org/prisons
Human Rights Watch conducts specialized prison research and campaigns for prisoners' rights, with the goal of focusing international attention on prison conditions worldwide.

National Commission on Correctional Health Care

http://www.ncchc.org

The NCCHC evaluates and develops policies related to health care services provided by detention facilities.

National Correctional Industry Association

http://www.nationalcia.org

The NCIA is an international nonprofit professional association, with a mission of promoting "excellence and credibility in correctional industries through professional development and innovative business solutions."

National Institute of Corrections

http://www.nicic.org

The NIC is an agency within the U.S. Department of Justice, Federal Bureau of Prisons, charged with providing training, technical assistance, information services, and policy and program development assistance to federal, state, and local corrections agencies.

Cases and Statutes

Beard v. Banks, U.S. 126 S.Ct. 2572 (2006).

The U.S. Supreme Court upheld a Pennsylvania prison policy that restricted the reading materials of inmates in a long-term segregation unit. The Court reasoned that the reading restrictions were a reasonable way to try to modify the behavior of problem inmates.

Cooper v. Pate, 378 U.S. 546 (1964).

The U.S. Supreme Court reinstated the claims of an Illinois inmate who alleged he was discriminated against because of his Islamic beliefs. The case stands for the principle that inmates can claim a First Amendment violation for violation of their religious-liberty rights.

Cruz v. Beto, 405 U.S. 319 (1972).

In this decision, the U.S. Supreme Court ruled that Texas prison officials may have discriminated against a Texas inmate who alleged that officials targeted him because of his Buddhist religious beliefs. The case expanded on the principle articulated in *Cooper v. Pate.*

Cutter v. Wilkinson, 544 U.S. 709 (2005).

In this decision, the U.S. Supreme Court ruled that the Religious Land Use and Institutionalized Persons Act (RLUIPA) did not violate the Establishment Clause of the First Amendment. Ohio prison officials had argued that RLUIPA unconstitutionally advanced religion. The Court, however, viewed RLUIPA as a permissible legislative accommodation of religion.

Farmer v. Brennan, 511 U.S. 825 (1994).

In this decision, the U.S. Supreme Court ruled that prison officials may be liable under the Eighth Amendment for failing to protect inmates from a physical assault only if the officials know that inmates face substantial risk of serious harm, and if officials disregard that risk by failing to take reasonable measures.

Hope v. Pelzer, 536 U.S. 730 (2002).

In this decision, the U.S. Supreme Court ruled that Alabama prison officials violated an inmate's Eighth Amendment rights to be free from cruel and unusual punishment when they tied him to a hitching post for hours on end with no bathroom breaks.

Hudson v. McMillan, 503 U.S. 1 (1992).

In this decision, the U.S. Supreme Court ruled that prison officials might violate an inmate's Eighth Amendment right to be free from cruel and unusual punishment if they use excessive force on the inmate—even if the inmate does not suffer a serious physical injury.

Johnson v. Avery, 393 U.S. 483 (1969).

In this decision, the U.S. Supreme Court struck down a Tennessee prison policy prohibiting "jailhouse lawyers," particularly when the state provided no form of legal assistance to inmates.

Lee v. Washington, 390 U.S. 333 (1968).

In this decision, the U.S. Supreme Court ruled that racially segregated prisons violated the Equal Protection Clause of the Fourteenth Amendment.

Lewis v. Casey, 518 U.S. 343 (1996).

In this decision, the U.S. Supreme Court ruled that an Arizona inmate failed to show a violation of his constitutional rights simply because the prison law library was not up to date.

O'Lone v. Estate of Shabazz, 482 U.S. 342 (1987).

In this decision, the Court ruled that prison officials did violate the First Amendment by preventing Muslim inmates from attending a weekly religious service that conflicted with general prison work-schedule policies.

Overton v. Bazzetta, 539 U.S. 126 (2003).

In this decision, the U.S. Supreme Court upheld numerous inmate visitation restrictions put in place by the Michigan Department of Corrections. The Court ruled that prison officials had a rational basis for trying to curtail visitation, in part to prohibit the smuggling of contraband and to prohibit drug use.

Porter v. Nussle, 534 U.S. 516 (2002).

In this decision, the U.S. Supreme Court ruled that the Prison Litigation Reform Act's exhaustion requirement—requiring inmates to first plead their complaints to prison administration—applies to all inmates claims, even those involving excessive force.

Procunier v. Martinez, 416 U.S. 396 (1974).

In this decision, the U.S. Supreme Court ruled that regulation of inmate mail could be justified "only if it furthers an important or substantial governmental interest unrelated to the suppression of free expression, and the limitation is no greater than necessary or essential to protect that interest." Applying this standard, the court struck down a California prison regulation prohibiting correspondence between inmates and noninmates that "unduly complain," "magnify grievances," or "express inflammatory political, racial, religious, or other views or beliefs."

Rhodes v. Chapman, 452 U.S. 337 (1981)

In this decision, the U.S. Supreme Court ruled that an Ohio prison policy of "double celling" (placing two inmates in a single-person cell) does not constitute cruel and unusual punishment within the meaning of the Eighth Amendment.

Ruffin v. Commonwealth, 62 Va. 790 (1871).

In this decision, the Supreme Court of Virginia ruled that an inmate was nothing more than a "slave of the state."

Shaw v. Murphy, 532 U.S. 223 (2001).

In this decision, the U.S. Supreme Court ruled that an inmate did not have a special First Amendment right to assist other inmates with their legal matters.

Thornburgh v. Abbott, 490 U.S. 401 (1989).

In this decision, the U.S. Supreme Court upheld federal prison regulations regulating inmate subscriptions. The Court ruled that the regulations, which allowed prison officials to prohibit inmate access to any publication deemed harmful to institutional security, were rationally related to prison security.

Turner v. Safley, 482 U.S. 78 (1987).

In this decision, the U.S. Supreme Court established that prison officials do not violate an inmate's constitutional rights as long as they have a reasonable penological justification (such as safety) for their actions. Applying this standard, the court struck down an inmate marriage restriction but upheld restrictions on inmates sending mail to other inmates.

Terms and Concepts

conditions of confinement
cruel and unusual punishment
deliberate indifference
Eighth Amendment
evolving standards of decency
exhaustion of administrative remedies
excessive force
First Amendment
Free Exercise Clause
Prison Litigation Reform Act
Religious Freedom Restoration Act
Religious Land Use and Institutionalized Persons Act

Beginning Legal Research

The goal of POINT/COUNTERPOINT is not only to provide the reader with an introduction to a controversial issue affecting society, but also to encourage the reader to explore the issue more fully. This appendix, then, is meant to serve as a guide to the reader in researching the current state of the law as well as exploring some of the public-policy arguments as to why existing laws should be changed or new laws are needed.

Like many types of research, legal research has become much faster and more accessible with the invention of the Internet. This appendix discusses some of the best starting points, but of course "surfing the Net" will uncover endless additional sources of information—some more reliable than others. Some important sources of law are not yet available on the Internet, but these can generally be found at the larger public and university libraries. Librarians usually are happy to point patrons in the right direction.

The most important source of law in the United States is the Constitution. Originally enacted in 1787, the Constitution outlines the structure of our federal government and sets limits on the types of laws that the federal government and state governments can pass. Through the centuries, a number of amendments have been added to or changed in the Constitution, most notably the first ten amendments, known collectively as the Bill of Rights, which guarantee important civil liberties. Each state also has its own constitution, many of which are similar to the U.S. Constitution. It is important to be familiar with the U.S. Constitution because so many of our laws are affected by its requirements. State constitutions often provide protections of individual rights that are even stronger than those set forth in the U.S. Constitution.

Within the guidelines of the U.S. Constitution, Congress—both the House of Representatives and the Senate—passes bills that are either vetoed or signed into law by the president. After the passage of the law, it becomes part of the United States Code, which is the official compilation of federal laws. The state legislatures use a similar process, in which bills become law when signed by the state's governor. Each state has its own official set of laws, some of which are published by the state and some of which are published by commercial publishers. The U.S. Code and the state codes are an important source of legal research; generally, legislators make efforts to make the language of the law as clear as possible.

However, reading the text of a federal or state law generally provides only part of the picture. In the American system of government, after the legislature passes laws and the executive (U.S. president or state governor) signs them, it is up to the judicial branch of the government, the court system, to interpret the laws and decide whether they violate any provision of the Constitution. At the state level, each state's supreme court has the ultimate authority in determining what a law means and whether or not it violates the state constitution. However, the federal courts—headed by the U.S. Supreme Court—can review state laws and court decisions to determine whether they violate federal laws or the U.S. Constitution. For example, a state court may find that a particular criminal law is valid under the state's constitution, but a federal court may then review the state court's decision and determine that the law is invalid under the U.S. Constitution.

It is important, then, to read court decisions when doing legal research. The Constitution uses language that is intentionally very general—for example, prohibiting "unreasonable searches and seizures" by the police—and court cases often provide more guidance. For example, the U.S. Supreme Court's 2001 decision in *Kyllo v. United States* held that scanning the outside of a person's house using a heat sensor to determine whether the person is growing marijuana is unreasonable—*if* it is done without a search warrant secured from a judge. Supreme Court decisions provide the most definitive explanation of the law of the land, and it is therefore important to include these in research. Often, when the Supreme Court has not decided a case on a particular issue, a decision by a federal appeals court or a state supreme court can provide guidance; but just as laws and constitutions can vary from state to state, so can federal courts be split on a particular interpretation of federal law or the U.S. Constitution. For example, federal appeals courts in Louisiana and California may reach opposite conclusions in similar cases.

Lawyers and courts refer to statutes and court decisions through a formal system of citations. Use of these citations reveals which court made the decision (or which legislature passed the statute) and when and enables the reader to locate the statute or court case quickly in a law library. For example, the legendary Supreme Court case *Brown v. Board of Education* has the legal citation 347 U.S. 483 (1954). At a law library, this 1954 decision can be found on page 483 of volume 347 of the U.S. Reports, the official collection of the Supreme Court's decisions. Citations can also be helpful in locating court cases on the Internet.

Understanding the current state of the law leads only to a partial understanding of the issues covered by the POINT/COUNTERPOINT series. For a fuller understanding of the issues, it is necessary to look at public-policy arguments that the current state of the law is not adequately addressing the issue.

Many groups lobby for new legislation or changes to existing legislation; the National Rifle Association (NRA), for example, lobbies Congress and the state legislatures constantly to make existing gun control laws less restrictive and not to pass additional laws. The NRA and other groups dedicated to various causes might also intervene in pending court cases: a group such as Planned Parenthood might file a brief amicus curiae (as "a friend of the court")—called an "amicus brief"—in a lawsuit that could affect abortion rights. Interest groups also use the media to influence public opinion, issuing press releases and frequently appearing in interviews on news programs and talk shows. The books in POINT/COUNTERPOINT list some of the interest groups that are active in the issue at hand, but in each case there are countless other groups working at the local, state, and national levels. It is important to read everything with a critical eye, for sometimes interest groups present information in a way that can be read only to their advantage. The informed reader must always look for bias.

Finding sources of legal information on the Internet is relatively simple thanks to "portal" sites such as FindLaw (*www.findlaw.com*), which provides access to a variety of constitutions, statutes, court opinions, law review articles, news articles, and other resources—including all Supreme Court decisions issued since 1893. Other useful sources of information include the U.S. Government Printing Office (*www.gpo.gov*), which contains a complete copy of the U.S. Code, and the Library of Congress's THOMAS system (*thomas.loc.gov*), which offers access to bills pending before Congress as well as recently passed laws. Of course, the Internet changes every second of every day, so it is best to do some independent searching. Most cases, studies, and opinions that are cited or referred to in public debate can be found online—and *everything* can be found in one library or another.

The Internet can provide a basic understanding of most important legal issues, but not all sources can be found there. To find some documents it is necessary to visit the law library of a university or a public law library; some cities have public law libraries, and many library systems keep legal documents at the main branch. On the following page are some common citation forms.

COMMON CITATION FORMS

Source of Law	Sample Citation	Notes
U.S. Supreme Court	*Employment Division v. Smith*, 485 U.S. 660 (1988)	The U.S. Reports is the official record of Supreme Court decisions. There is also an unofficial Supreme Court ("S. Ct.") reporter.
U.S. Court of Appeals	*United States v. Lambert*, 695 F.2d 536 (11th Cir. 1983)	Appellate cases appear in the Federal Reporter, designated by "F." The 11th Circuit has jurisdiction in Alabama, Florida, and Georgia.
U.S. District Court	*Carillon Importers, Ltd. v. Frank Pesce Group, Inc.*, 913 F.Supp. 1559 (S.D.Fla. 1996)	Federal trial-level decisions are reported in the Federal Supplement ("F. Supp."). Some states have multiple federal districts; this case originated in the Southern District of Florida.
U.S. Code	Thomas Jefferson Commemoration Commission Act, 36 U.S.C., §149 (2002)	Sometimes the popular names of legislation—names with which the public may be familiar—are included with the U.S. Code citation.
State Supreme Court	*Sterling v. Cupp*, 290 Ore. 611, 614, 625 P.2d 123, 126 (1981)	The Oregon Supreme Court decision is reported in both the state's reporter and the Pacific regional reporter.
State Statute	Pennsylvania Abortion Control Act of 1982, 18 Pa. Cons. Stat. 3203-3220 (1990)	States use many different citation formats for their statutes.

PICTURE CREDITS

page:

13: Associated Press
27: AP Images, Rich Pedroncelli
53: AP Images, STF

63: AP Images, Jeff Robbins
85: Associated Press

cover: AP Images, Stephen Morton

DAVID L. HUDSON, Jr., is an author-attorney who has published widely on First Amendment and other constitutional law issues. Hudson is a research attorney with the First Amendment Center at Vanderbilt University and a First Amendment contributing editor to the American Bar Association's *Preview of the United States Supreme Court Cases.* He obtained his undergraduate degree from Duke University and his law degree from Vanderbilt University Law School.

ALAN MARZILLI, M.A., J.D., lives in Washington, D.C., and is a program associate with Advocates for Human Potential, Inc., a research and consulting firm based in Sudbury, Mass., and Albany, N.Y. He primarily works on developing training and educational materials for agencies of the federal government on topics such as housing, mental health policy, employment, and transportation. He has spoken on mental health issues in 30 states, the District of Columbia, and Puerto Rico; his work has included training mental health administrators, nonprofit management and staff, and people with mental illnesses and their families on a wide variety of topics, including effective advocacy, community-based mental health services, and housing. He has written several handbooks and training curricula that are used nationally and as far away as the territory of Guam. He managed statewide and national mental health advocacy programs and worked for several public interest lobbying organizations while studying law at Georgetown University. He has written more than a dozen books, including numerous titles in the POINT/COUNTERPOINT series.